The Parthian Empire

The Rise and Fall of Rome's Eastern Rival, the Arsacid Dynasty, and the Roman–Parthian Wars

Samuel Corwin

Table Of Contents

Introduction:

The Empire Rome Could Not Break

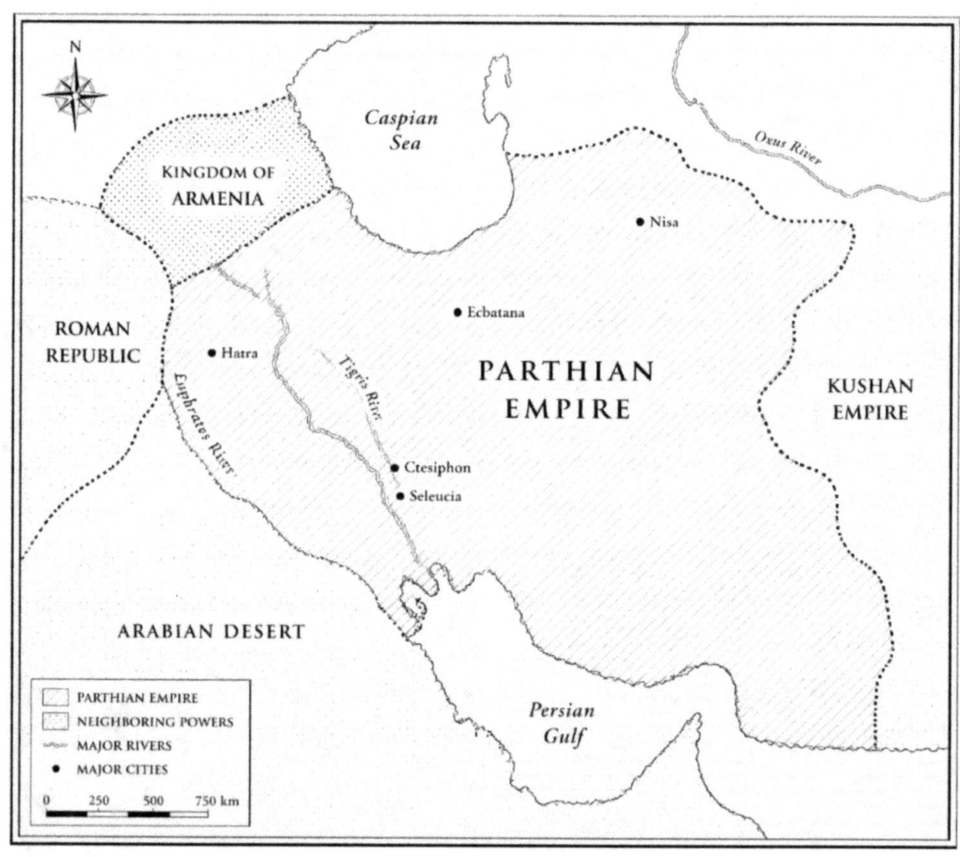

The Parthian Empire, c. 60 BCE

On a blistering June morning in 53 BCE, forty thousand Roman soldiers stood sweating in the desert south of a town called Carrhae, waiting for an enemy they did not understand. By nightfall, most of them would be dead, dying, or in chains. Their commander's severed head would soon be used as a stage prop in a Greek tragedy performed at a Parthian court.

It was the worst military disaster Rome had suffered in a century, and the empire that inflicted it is one most readers have never heard of. For nearly five hundred years, a dynasty of horse-riding kings governed a territory stretching from the Euphrates to the Hindu Kush. They fought Rome to a standstill, brokered the trade that became known as the Silk Road, and shaped the religious and political life of western Asia. Then they vanished from the story we tell ourselves about the ancient world. This book is an attempt to bring them back. It begins, as their collision with the West began, in the dust outside Carrhae, where a Roman triumvir learned what every ambitious general after him would have to reckon with: that east of the Euphrates lay a power that could not be broken by legions alone. Understanding why that was true - and why we have forgotten it - is the first step in recovering the empire Rome could not conquer.

A Lost Superpower

Marcus Licinius Crassus was the richest man in Rome, and he wanted more. He had crushed the slave revolt of Spartacus, bankrolled the careers of Pompey and Caesar, and now, at sixty, he wanted the one prize his partners in the First Triumvirate had already won for themselves: military glory on a world-historical scale. Caesar had Gaul. Pompey had the East. Crassus would take Parthia.

In the spring of 54 BCE he crossed the Euphrates at the head of seven legions. The campaign was, on paper, straightforward. Roman heavy infantry had conquered Macedonians, Carthaginians, Gauls, and Greeks. Parthia was, to Roman eyes, simply another Hellenistic kingdom waiting to be peeled open. What no one in the Roman command seems to have understood was that the Parthians did not fight like any enemy Rome had faced before.

The man who met them was named Surena. He was not a king - he was a nobleman in his early thirties commanding the household troops of the Parthian monarch Orodes II - but he had done his homework. He led a force perhaps a quarter the size of Crassus's, and it contained almost no infantry. What it had instead was cavalry of two kinds: light horse archers who could loose arrows at full gallop, and cataphracts, armored lancers on armored horses, men and mounts encased head to hoof in scale and mail. Surena also brought a baggage train of a thousand camels. The camels were carrying arrows.

On June 9, 53 BCE, the two armies met on flat, open ground near the town of Carrhae, in what is now southeastern Turkey. The Romans formed their famous hollow square. The Parthian horse archers began to circle, shooting inward, and did not stop. When the Romans charged, the archers wheeled away and kept shooting backward over their horses' rumps - the maneuver that would be remembered in European languages for two thousand years as the Parthian shot. When the legionaries locked shields and hunkered down, the cataphracts came crashing in at a walk, then a trot, then a thundering charge that punched through the Roman line like an iron fist through wet clay. When Publius Crassus took the cavalry out to drive the archers off, they lured him away from the main army, surrounded him, and killed him. His head was brought back to his father on the point of a spear.

By the time the sun set, perhaps twenty thousand Romans were dead. Ten thousand more would be taken prisoner and marched east to the Parthian frontier town of Merv, where their descendants were still being noted by travelers a generation later. Crassus himself died the next morning, killed during botched surrender negotiations. The aquilae, the sacred legionary eagles, were carried off as trophies. Only about ten thousand Romans stumbled back across the Euphrates to Syria.

In Rome, the disaster was nearly unspeakable. The shattering of the Triumvirate it caused would help push the republic into the civil war that produced Caesar's dictatorship and, eventually, the empire of Augustus. For decades afterward, recovering the lost eagles became a Roman obsession - so much so that when Augustus finally negotiated their return in 20 BCE, he put the event on his coinage and celebrated it as if it were a victory. It was not a victory. It was a treaty, between two empires that had taken each other's measure and decided, for now, to coexist.

That is the first thing to understand about the Parthians. For nearly three centuries, from the 60s BCE to the 220s CE, they were not Rome's barbarian neighbor. They were Rome's peer.

Why the Parthians Vanished from Memory

If the Parthians were so formidable, why does almost no one know their name?

Part of the answer is simple geography of memory. The story of the ancient Mediterranean world has been told, for centuries, by the heirs of Rome. European schoolchildren learned Latin, read Caesar and Cicero, and absorbed a map of antiquity on which civilization thinned and dimmed the farther east one traveled. Beyond the Euphrates, on the Roman mental map, lay a zone of rumor: rich, dangerous, vaguely oriental, inhabited by kings with hard-to-pronounce names. The Parthians were cast as the shadowy antagonists of a drama whose protagonists were always in the west.

Part of the answer is the peculiar tragedy of Iranian historiography. When the Sasanian dynasty overthrew the last Parthian king, Artabanus IV, in 224 CE, they set about systematically erasing their predecessors from the official record. The Sasanians considered themselves the true heirs of the old

Achaemenid Persians of Cyrus and Darius; the Parthians, in their telling, had been a five-century interregnum of petty, squabbling warlords. This propaganda worked. By the time the great Persian epic the *Shahnameh* was composed in the tenth century, the Parthian centuries had been compressed into a handful of vague paragraphs about the "tribal kings." Nearly half a millennium of history had been, quite deliberately, forgotten at home.

Part of the answer is that the Parthians did not write much about themselves - or, if they did, little has survived. They were a culture built around oral tradition, court poetry recited by minstrels called *gosan*, and the spoken word of a warrior aristocracy. Their administrative records were kept on perishable materials. Their own histories, if ever written down in the form the Greeks and Romans would have recognized, have not come down to us. What remains is scattered: coins, a handful of inscriptions, a few parchment documents from a dry corner of the empire, archaeological traces of cities buried under later settlements.

Part of the answer lies in the nineteenth and early twentieth centuries, when the modern discipline of ancient history was being built alongside European empire in the Middle East. British, French, and German scholars brought home the monuments of Egypt, Mesopotamia, and Achaemenid Persia by the shipload. But the Parthians fit awkwardly into the categories on offer. They were not satisfyingly "classical" like the Greeks, not satisfyingly "oriental-despotic" like the Achaemenids, not conveniently biblical like the Assyrians. For the taxonomies of Victorian scholarship, they were a problem. And so, quietly, they were shelved.

The result is a strange vacancy in the middle of the map. We know Julius Caesar and we know Cleopatra. We know Augustus and we know Herod. Across the Euphrates from all of them stood a vast, sophisticated empire whose kings corresponded with Rome as equals, and most educated readers today could not name a single one of them.

Sources, Silences, and the Problem of Writing Parthian History

Writing a history of the Parthians is, in practical terms, a matter of working out what can be said honestly from evidence that is almost entirely produced by their enemies, their successors, or the silent testimony of objects in the ground.

Start with the literary sources. The fullest narrative accounts of Parthian history are in Greek and Latin. Plutarch, writing more than a century after Carrhae, gives us the most vivid description of the battle - and of Surena, whom he portrays with a kind of awed hostility as tall, beautiful, and cunning. Cassius Dio, Tacitus, Josephus, and a scattering of others provide episodes, usually from the perspective of Roman frontier politics. These writers are often well-informed, sometimes extraordinarily so, but they share a common limitation: they are interested in Parthia only when Parthia touches Rome. Decades of internal Parthian history can pass in their pages without a sentence, only to surge back into focus when a Parthian army crosses the Euphrates or a Parthian prince turns up in exile at a Roman court.

The Chinese sources offer a different and precious perspective. In the *Shiji* of Sima Qian and the *Hanshu* of Ban Gu, Parthia appears as *Anxi*, a wealthy and orderly kingdom that sits astride the overland routes west of Central Asia. Chinese envoys, traders, and geographers took careful notes. They describe Parthian cities, coinage, administrative practices, and the strange habit of the Parthians of writing horizontally on leather rather than vertically on bamboo. For any historian trying to see the empire from outside the Roman gaze, these eastern texts are indispensable.

Then there is the material record, which has grown enormously in the last century. Coins are the workhorses of Parthian chronology: more than thirty kings issued silver drachms and tetradrachms stamped with Greek inscriptions and portraits, and the sequence of their issues allows numismatists to reconstruct a dynastic framework that the literary sources cannot. Excavations at Nisa, the old dynastic heartland in what is now Turkmenistan, have produced thousands of ostraca - inked potsherds recording deliveries of wine to the royal estates - that offer a rare glimpse into Parthian administration in the Parthians' own language. Dura-Europos, a Parthian-then-Roman frontier city on the middle Euphrates, has yielded temples, houses, paintings, and legal documents that illuminate everyday life in the contact zone. Sites in Iran and Iraq - Hatra, Ctesiphon, Seleucia-on-the-Tigris, Susa - fill in more.

The historian's task is to triangulate. A notice in Tacitus can be checked against a dated coin. A Chinese description of a royal ceremony can be set beside a relief carving from a Parthian temple. An ostracon from Nisa, casually noting that such-and-such a vintage came from the vineyard of a prince, can anchor a name the Roman sources mention only once.

None of this produces the kind of history one can write about Augustan Rome, where a literate elite left letters, speeches, poems, and autobiographies by the shelf-load. The Parthians remain, in important ways, a quieter people. We do not know what most of their kings sounded like. We do not have a single surviving work of Parthian literature in its original form. There are years in the middle of the first century CE when we cannot say with confidence who was sitting on the throne.

What we do have is enough to reconstruct, with care, the outline of an empire: its political institutions, its military system, its religious life, its economic reach, its dynastic quarrels, its long cold war with Rome and its shifting relations with the steppe, with India, and with Han China. It is a history told through gaps, in which the historian must sometimes say honestly, "Here the evidence runs out." Where the sources conflict - and on crucial questions such as the succession of kings in the first century BCE, or the nature of the office Surena held, they often do - the responsible course is to say so.

Readers of this book will find those uncertainties flagged, not papered over. The point is not to pretend to a confidence the evidence does not support. The point is to show that even with all the silences, there is an extraordinary story here.

What This Book Will Recover

The ambition of this book is to put the Parthians back where they belong: at the center of the ancient world, not at its edge.

That means, first, taking their military achievement seriously. Carrhae was not a fluke. The Parthian way of war - the combination of horse archer and cataphract, the use of feigned retreat, the mastery of logistics across vast distances - was a coherent tactical system that held the Roman frontier on the Euphrates for nearly three centuries. Every major Roman counterstrike eastward, from Mark Antony's catastrophic Armenian campaign in 36 BCE to Trajan's brilliant and ultimately futile invasion in 115 CE, ran into the same problem. Rome could win battles in Parthia. It could not hold Parthia.

Second, the Parthians deserve to be understood as state-builders, not merely as warriors. They governed a mosaic of peoples - Iranian, Semitic, Greek, Armenian, Arab, Indian - through a system of layered authority that combined a strong royal court with a network of vassal kingdoms and powerful aristocratic clans. They kept Greek as a language of coinage and administration for centuries after they had displaced the Greeks politically. They tolerated, in a way that few ancient states did, an extraordinary religious pluralism: Zoroastrians, Jews, Buddhists, pagans of every description, and eventually Christians all flourished under Parthian rule.

Third, the Parthians were the indispensable middlemen of Eurasian commerce. The Silk Road - that modern shorthand for the exchange of goods, technologies, and ideas between China and the Mediterranean - ran through Parthian territory. Parthian merchants, Parthian customs officials, Parthian caravan cities made the system work. When a Roman senator's wife wore Chinese silk, she wore it because the Parthians let it cross their empire, and took a cut along the way.

Finally, there is the question of what the long Parthian peace - a peace punctuated by wars but never shattered by collapse - can tell us about how empires actually survive. The Parthians did not build the tightest bureaucracy in the ancient world. They did not have the best roads or the largest standing army. What they had was flexibility: a willingness to let local elites govern locally, to absorb rather than erase conquered cultures, to bend rather than break. For almost five hundred years, that was enough.

A Map of the Journey Ahead

The chapters that follow trace the Parthian empire from its obscure beginnings to its sudden fall, and they can be read as a single narrative or sampled in pieces.

Part One returns to origins. It follows a tribe of horse-riding Parni, moving south out of the Central Asian steppe in the middle of the third century BCE, as they seize a rebellious satrapy from the collapsing Seleucid empire in 247 BCE and plant the dynasty that would rule for nearly five centuries. It introduces Arsaces, the founder whose name every subsequent king would take as a throne-title, and it asks how a small band of steppe warriors became the masters of Iran.

Part Two examines the long rise under the great kings of the second and first centuries BCE - above all Mithridates I, who conquered Mesopotamia, and Mithridates II, who first opened diplomatic relations with Han China and with Rome. Here the Parthian state took its mature form: the court at Ctesiphon, the council of noble clans, the cavalry army, the multilingual administration.

Part Three is about Rome. Carrhae, Antony's disaster, the long diplomatic dance under Augustus and his successors, the wars of Trajan and Lucius

Verus, the rhythm of invasion and stalemate on the Euphrates. It is the part of Parthian history best documented in the western sources, and the part most often misunderstood.

Part Four turns eastward and inward: the Silk Road, the religious ferment, the cities, the private lives we can glimpse through documents and excavation. Here we meet Parthian women of power, Jewish communities that thrived under Arsacid protection, Buddhist monks who crossed the empire bound for China, and merchants whose account books survive in fragments.

Part Five tells the story of the fall - the civil wars, the revolt of Ardashir of Persis, the battle of Hormozdgan in 224 CE that ended the dynasty, and the long Sasanian campaign of memory-erasure that followed. It closes by tracing what the Parthians left behind: in Iranian culture, in the military systems of their successors, in the Roman imagination, and in the physical infrastructure of the Silk Road that outlived them by a thousand years.

Quick Summary

- At Carrhae in 53 BCE, a Parthian force under Surena destroyed a Roman army of 40,000 led by Crassus, killing roughly 20,000 and capturing 10,000.
- The Parthian Empire ruled a vast territory from the Euphrates to the Hindu Kush for nearly five centuries, from 247 BCE to 224 CE.
- Parthian military power rested on a combination of mounted horse archers and armored cataphract lancers, a system Rome could never fully counter.
- The Parthians were largely erased from memory by the Sasanian dynasty that overthrew them and by the Rome-centered tradition of Western historiography.

- Most surviving written sources are Greek, Roman, or Chinese - outsider accounts - supplemented by coins, inscriptions, and archaeology.
- The empire was religiously pluralist, administratively layered, and economically central to the Silk Road trade between Han China and the Mediterranean.
- Rome and Parthia coexisted as peer empires for nearly three centuries, a relationship of rivalry, diplomacy, and occasional catastrophic war.

The Parthians are not a footnote to Roman history. They are half of a story that, told from only one side, has never made full sense. The legions that marched east from Syria did not march into a void. They marched into the territory of an empire as coherent, ambitious, and self-aware as their own - an empire that had taken the measure of Rome, and found it wanting. To recover the Parthians is to recover the world as it actually was: not a Mediterranean dominated by a single rising power, but a Eurasia balanced between two. The rest of this book is about the empire on the other side of that balance, and about the riders whose names Rome could not forget, even when the rest of us did.

Before the Parthians could humble Crassus in the desert, they had to become Parthians at all. The riders whose arrows darkened the sky at Carrhae were the distant heirs of a much smaller people, a tribe on the edge of a crumbling Greek world, whose first claim to kingship was little more than a leather cap and an ambition. To understand how an empire took Rome's measure and found it wanting, we have to go back almost two centuries earlier, to the grasslands east of the Caspian, where the story properly begins.

Chapter 1:

Out of the Steppe

In 247 BCE, a chieftain whose name we barely know pulled a leather cap onto his head and claimed a kingdom he did not yet possess. Five centuries later, his descendants would be negotiating as equals with Roman emperors. The distance between those two facts is the subject of this book.

The Parthians did not begin as Parthians at all. They began as the Parni, one tribe among several in a loose confederation called the Dahae, riders of the dry grasslands east of the Caspian Sea. They spoke an Iranian language, buried their dead with horse tack, and owed nothing to the Greek-speaking kings who claimed dominion over their pastures from distant palaces in Syria. How such a people came to seize a province, found a dynasty, and outlast the Seleucid Empire that once towered over them is a story about timing, terrain, and a particular kind of political imagination. It is also a story that starts not with armies, but with the slow erosion of someone else's empire. When the Parni descended into the satrapy of Parthia in the middle of the third century BCE, they were not conquering a thriving kingdom. They were walking into a house whose roof had already begun to fall in.

The Dahae Confederation and the Parni

The steppe that stretches east from the Caspian Sea is not a single terrain but a gradient - from salt flats and reed marshes near the shoreline, through scrub and feather grass, rising eventually into the foothills of the Kopet Dag. It is country built for horses and for people willing to move with them. Here, by the fourth and third centuries BCE, lived a confederation that Greek and Roman writers called the Dahae.

The Dahae were not a state. They were an alliance of pastoral tribes sharing language, ritual, and the practical arrangements of a life on the move. Ancient authors generally name three constituent groups, among them the Parni - sometimes rendered Aparni - whose territory lay along the Ochus River, in the hinterland of what is now Turkmenistan. They spoke an eastern dialect of Iranian, related to but distinct from the Persian of the old Achaemenid heartland. Their religion we can only glimpse: ancestral spirits, sky gods, the ritual importance of fire and horses, a cosmology probably akin to the Zoroastrianism taking firmer shape among their settled cousins to the south, but less codified, more local, more tied to the rhythms of the herd.

What set the Parni apart - what set all the steppe peoples apart - was the horse. A Parni boy learned to ride before he learned to fight, and he learned to fight from the saddle. The characteristic weapon was the composite bow, a short, recurved instrument of wood, horn, and sinew, capable of punching an arrow through armor at fifty paces. Fired from a galloping mount by a man who could twist in the saddle and loose backward over his horse's rump - the move the Romans would later call the Parthian shot - it was one of the deadliest weapons in the ancient world.

For the settled empires to the south, such peoples were a permanent problem. The Achaemenid Persians had pushed fortified lines against the Dahae. Alexander had recruited from them as auxiliaries on his march east. The Seleucids who inherited Alexander's eastern territories continued both policies, alternately fighting and hiring the tribesmen of the steppe fringe. Some Parni served in Seleucid armies. Some watched, and remembered the routes.

By the 250s BCE, the Parni were led by a figure our sources call Arsaces. Whether this was a personal name, a title, or both is uncertain - later Parthian kings would all take the throne name Arsaces, in a gesture of dynastic fidelity that has driven historians to despair. What seems clear is that he commanded a coherent war band, probably a few thousand mounted fighters with their families and herds, and that he was watching the kingdom to his south with an attentive eye. Across the Kopet Dag mountains, in the Seleucid satrapy of Parthia, something was coming loose.

The Seleucid World in the Third Century BCE

Alexander the Great died in Babylon in 323 BCE, and for the next forty years his generals fought over the pieces. By the 280s, the dust had settled enough to see the outlines. Ptolemy's family held Egypt. The Antigonids held Macedon. And a Macedonian officer named Seleucus, who had served as a junior commander under Alexander, had assembled the largest prize of all: a sprawling realm that stretched, at its height, from the Mediterranean coast of Syria to the edge of the Indus Valley.

The Seleucid Empire was an improbable creation. It had no natural center, no shared language among its subjects, no single religion, and no organic unity beyond the fact that its ruling class was Greek and Macedonian and its army was built around the phalanx of long-spearmen that Alexander had made famous. What held it together was the road network inherited from the Persians, a scatter of Greek colonial cities with names like Antioch and Seleucia, and the personal energy of the king.

Personal energy, however, is a finite resource. By the reign of Antiochus II, who came to the throne in 261 BCE, the empire was stretched across too many fronts. In the west, the Seleucids fought a grinding series of wars with Ptolemaic Egypt over control of the Syrian coast - the so-called Syrian Wars, which drained treasuries and armies through the middle decades of the century. In Anatolia, local dynasts and the rising kingdom of Pergamon were chipping at the edges. To the north, the Galatian Celts who had crossed into Asia Minor in the 270s remained a chronic irritant.

The east, meanwhile, was taken for granted. The old satrapies of Media, Parthia, Hyrcania, Aria, and Bactria had been brought back under Seleucid control in the late fourth century and were administered by satraps appointed from the court. They paid tribute, supplied soldiers when asked, and were expected to look after themselves. This was workable when the king's attention, and his armies, could be swung eastward at need. It became dangerous when the king's attention was permanently elsewhere.

Around 245 BCE - the chronology is vexed, and historians differ on the exact sequence - two of those eastern satraps decided that the center was no longer strong enough to discipline them. Diodotus, the satrap of Bactria, the rich province on the upper Oxus, began minting coins in his own name and styling himself king. A little to the west, Andragoras, the satrap of Parthia, did the same. The Seleucid east, from the Caspian to the Hindu Kush, slipped its leash.

For Seleucus II, who inherited the throne in 246 BCE amid a fresh war with Egypt and a civil war with his own brother, there was simply no bandwidth to respond. The eastern provinces would have to be recovered later. Much later, as it turned out. In the meantime, a vacuum had opened in the corridor between Bactria and the Caspian - and on the far side of the Kopet Dag, the Parni were saddling their horses.

Arsaces I and the Seizure of Parthia

The satrapy of Parthia, in the mid-third century BCE, was a crescent of irrigated land tucked between the steppe to the north and the salt desert of the Dasht-e Kavir to the south. Its heart was the fertile strip along the southern slopes of the Kopet Dag, watered by streams running off the mountains. Its capital was Hecatompylos, the City of a Hundred Gates, somewhere in the vicinity of modern Damghan. Its population was mostly Iranian-speaking peasants and herders, salted with Greek colonists in a handful of planted towns. Not a rich province, but a strategic one: the road from Seleucia to Bactria ran through it, and whoever held Parthia controlled the hinge of the empire.

When Andragoras declared his independence from Seleucus II, he inherited all these advantages. He also inherited all the problems. His Greek garrisons were small. His legitimacy, such as it was, rested on being the man the old empire had appointed - a weak claim once he had renounced the old empire. He could not count on reinforcement from the west, because the west was occupied, but he could not count on loyalty from the east either, because his neighbor Diodotus in Bactria was a rival and not a friend. Andragoras was, in every practical sense, alone.

Arsaces moved in 247 BCE, or perhaps a year or two later - the Parthians would later fix their era on 247, counting the years of their empire from that date, and the round number has the smell of a retrospective tidying. What the sources describe, with some variation, is a two-stage operation. First, the Parni crossed the Kopet Dag and established themselves in the northern part of Parthia, the region called Astauene. Then, in a second campaign that may have taken several years, they moved south, defeated Andragoras in battle - he is reported to have been killed - and took Hecatompylos itself. By around 238 BCE, Arsaces controlled the old satrapy from end to end.

He did not stop there. In the same years, or shortly after, Arsaces pushed west into Hyrcania, the fertile province along the southeastern corner of the Caspian. This gave him a second agricultural base, access to the forested slopes of the Elburz, and a buffer against any Seleucid army marching east along the great trunk road. It also gave him something more abstract but more important: a recognizable kingdom with borders, towns, and tax revenues - something that could be defended and passed on.

What Arsaces did next mattered more than the conquest itself. He did not sack the cities. He did not massacre the Greek colonists or drive out the local elites. He took over the Seleucid administrative machinery he found on the ground - the scribes, the tax collectors, the mint at Hecatompylos - and put it to work for himself. His first coins, struck in Greek style with Greek legends, show a seated archer in nomadic dress on the reverse. The imagery is precise: the archer is a Parni, the coin is a Seleucid convention, and the message is that the new king intends to be both.

It was a shrewd choice, and it set the template for everything that followed. Arsaces had arrived from the steppe, but he did not intend to rule as a raider. He intended to rule as a king, with all the furniture that Greek and Persian tradition had developed for the purpose. The Parni chieftain was on his way to becoming a shah.

Nomad Kingship and Early Arsacid Identity

One of the enduring puzzles of the Arsacid dynasty is what kind of kingship its founders thought they were practicing. The answer, as best we can reconstruct it, is: several kinds at once.

From the steppe, Arsaces brought the habits of nomadic leadership. A chief led because his warriors followed him; they followed him because he provided success, plunder, and a share of the pasture. Kingship in this tradition was personal and contingent. It was bound up with the war band, the extended family, and the horse. Legitimacy ran through a line of ancestors, but it also had to be earned in every generation. A king who lost battles could expect to lose followers. A king who won could expect to accumulate them.

From the settled world the Parni had now entered, Arsaces inherited a very different model. The Achaemenid Persians, two centuries before, had developed an elaborate ideology of kingship: the monarch as the chosen of Ahura Mazda, the ordainer of justice, the keeper of the land's prosperity. The Seleucids had grafted onto this a Hellenistic overlay - the king as quasi-divine benefactor, the giver of cities, the subject of cult. Both traditions assumed a scale of rule and a permanence of institution quite foreign to the tent.

Arsaces and his immediate successors borrowed from all of this, selectively. They kept the steppe habit of calling every king Arsaces, folding individual identity into a dynastic one - a practice probably meant to assert the unbroken legitimacy of the line. They adopted the title of king, and eventually King of Kings, with its Achaemenid resonance. They maintained a mobile court, traveling between summer and winter capitals, preserving the nomadic reflex even from fixed palaces. They patronized Greek cities and struck coins in Greek. They also protected fire temples and claimed descent, later if not at first, from the old Achaemenid royal house.

The result was a hybrid, and the hybridity was the point. The Arsacids would never pretend to be purely Iranian, purely Greek, or purely anything else. They ruled a realm that contained all these pieces, and they offered each piece a version of themselves it could recognize. To their Parni kinsmen, the king remained a war chief on horseback. To the Greek cities of the plateau, he was a familiar Hellenistic monarch. To the Iranian peasantry, he was a successor to the Great Kings of old.

This flexibility was not a weakness, though later Roman observers sometimes read it as one. It was the central technology of Parthian rule.

The First Generations of Rule

Arsaces I died around 213 BCE, after a reign of roughly three and a half decades. He was succeeded by his son, Arsaces II - the name now a title - who inherited a kingdom that had grown fast and was about to be tested.

The test came from the west. Antiochus III, who had taken the Seleucid throne in 223 BCE, was the most energetic king his dynasty had produced in two generations, and he was determined to restore the empire his predecessors had let slip. After stabilizing the western frontier, he launched, beginning in 209 BCE, what ancient sources call his anabasis - a march east to recover the lost provinces. It was a deliberate echo of Alexander.

Antiochus came into Parthia in force. Arsaces II could not meet him in open battle; the Seleucid army, fielding its full phalanx and heavy cavalry, was simply too powerful. Instead, the Parthian king fell back on the steppe's oldest strategy: withdraw, harass, deny supplies, stretch the invader's lines. Antiochus pushed through to Hecatompylos. He crossed the Elburz into Hyrcania. He fought a series of hard engagements. By 206 BCE, he had made his point.

What he did not do - and this is the crucial fact - is depose the Arsacids. The settlement Antiochus imposed left Arsaces II on his throne as a Seleucid vassal, obliged to supply troops and acknowledge Seleucid overlordship, but substantially intact within his own realm. Antiochus needed to march on to Bactria and India, and he could not spare the men to garrison Parthia permanently. A compliant Arsacid was better than a destroyed one.

For the Parthians, the lesson was decisive. They had survived the return of Seleucid power. They had kept their dynasty, their capital, and the machinery of their state. When, a few years later, Antiochus's ambitions collapsed in the west - his defeat by Rome at Magnesia in 190 BCE - the pressure on the eastern frontier evaporated. The Arsacids, quietly, went back to expanding.

Key Figures & Events

- **Arsaces I (r. c. 247-213 BCE):** Parni chieftain who seized the satrapy of Parthia from Andragoras and founded the dynasty that would rule for nearly five centuries.
- **Andragoras (d. c. 238 BCE):** Last Seleucid satrap of Parthia; declared independence from Seleucus II and was killed in the Parni conquest.
- **Diodotus of Bactria:** Fellow rebel satrap whose parallel breakaway opened the strategic vacuum Arsaces exploited.

- **Arsaces II (r. c. 213-after 206 BCE):** Son and successor of the founder; survived Antiochus III's eastern campaign as a client king.
- **Antiochus III (r. 223-187 BCE):** Seleucid king whose anabasis of 209-204 BCE briefly reimposed suzerainty over Parthia without destroying the dynasty.

Analysis

Three factors came together in the middle decades of the third century BCE to make the Parthian rise possible, if not inevitable. First was Seleucid overstretch: an empire fighting in Syria and Anatolia simply could not project force beyond the Kopet Dag. Second was the quality of the Parni war band - mobile, disciplined, led by a chief shrewd enough to strike when the moment came and measured enough not to overreach. Third, and most underappreciated, was the Arsacid willingness to govern through institutions they had not built. Arsaces took Hecatompylos, but he kept its scribes. He wore nomad dress on his coins and struck them to Greek weight standards. He built a state by layering identities rather than replacing them.

That decision - to be many things at once - would define the empire for the next four and a half centuries. It would allow the Arsacids to hold a realm stretching from the Euphrates to the edge of the Hindu Kush, speaking a dozen languages and worshipping half the gods of the ancient world. It would also make them legible, simultaneously, to their subjects and to the rivals who would eventually come looking for them across the Syrian desert. The Romans, when they arrived, would find a kingdom that refused to fit any single category they understood. That was not a failure of Parthian clarity. That was the strategy.

Quick Summary

- The Parthians originated as the Parni, a tribe of the Dahae confederation on the steppe east of the Caspian Sea.

- The Seleucid Empire's wars in Syria and Anatolia left its eastern satrapies effectively unguarded by the 240s BCE.
- Around 247 BCE, the Parni chief Arsaces began a conquest that by 238 BCE delivered the satrapy of Parthia into his hands.
- Arsaces I killed the rebel satrap Andragoras and expanded into Hyrcania, preserving local administration rather than destroying it.
- Arsacid kingship blended steppe, Achaemenid, and Hellenistic traditions, producing a deliberately hybrid political identity.
- Antiochus III's eastern campaign of 209-204 BCE reimposed Seleucid suzerainty but left Arsaces II on his throne.
- After Antiochus's defeat by Rome at Magnesia in 190 BCE, Seleucid pressure on Parthia collapsed, freeing the Arsacids to expand.

In the space of two generations, a tribe of horsemen had become a dynasty. They had taken a crumbling province and turned it into a platform; they had faced the full weight of the Seleucid army and survived. What they did not yet know - what no one in the 190s BCE could know - was that the empire that had once loomed over them was entering its final phase, and that the road west, toward Mesopotamia and the ancient cities of the Tigris, was about to open. The riders from the steppe were about to become something their ancestors could scarcely have imagined: the successors of Cyrus, the heirs of Babylon, and the eastern counterweight to Rome.

The Parni had survived the Seleucids and settled into something more permanent than a chieftain's gamble. But surviving is not the same as ruling, and a strip of northeastern Iran is not yet an empire. The leap from frontier kingdom to Eurasian power required more than luck and horsemanship. It required a king willing to reach for Mesopotamia, to claim the mantle of Cyrus, and to press west while the Seleucid world finished bleeding out. In the middle of the second century BCE, the Arsacids found such a king, and everything changed.

Chapter 2:

Mithridates the Great and the Forging of an Empire

When Mithridates I came to the throne around 171 BCE, the Arsacids controlled a modest strip of northeastern Iran - a kingdom of horsemen clinging to the flank of a crumbling Greek world. By his death some three decades later, they ruled from the Euphrates to the edge of India. No one saw it coming.

Empires rarely announce themselves. They accumulate, quietly, in the gaps left by other people's misfortunes. In the middle of the second century BCE, the Seleucid dynasty - Alexander's bickering heirs in Syria and Iran - was bleeding from every seam. Usurpers murdered kings in Antioch. Satraps declared independence on the Iranian plateau. Greco-Bactrian rulers marched east into India chasing glory and left their home provinces lightly garrisoned. Into this vacuum stepped a man whose name most Roman schoolboys would never learn, though his work would frustrate Roman legions for the next three centuries. Mithridates I did not merely enlarge Parthia. He transformed a frontier chieftainship of the Arsacid line into a state that could, and did, claim the mantle of the Achaemenid Great Kings. What follows traces that transformation: the strategy, the campaigns, the crowning at Seleucia, and the deliberate resurrection of a title - King of Kings - that carried the weight of half a millennium.

A Strategic Revolution

To understand what Mithridates did, consider what he inherited. His predecessors had spent a century fighting simply to exist. Arsaces I had carved Parthia out of a rebellion against the Seleucid satrap Andragoras around 247 BCE. His successors defended that foothold against periodic Seleucid reconquest expeditions, the last of which, under Antiochus III, had forced the Arsacids into something close to vassalage. For decades, Parthian strategy had been reactive: absorb the blow, retreat into the steppe, wait out the storm. Mithridates reversed the polarity.

The shift was not only military but conceptual. The early Arsacids ruled as kings of a people - the Parni, a steppe clan that had settled among the Parthians and taken their name. Mithridates began to rule as a king of territory, of cities, of many peoples at once. This required new instruments. It required a standing core of cavalry that could be projected far from home pastures. It required administrators who could collect taxes in Aramaic, issue edicts in Greek, and speak to Iranian nobles in their own tongue. It required, above all, a willingness to think in decades rather than seasons.

Parthia's geography suited the ambition. The heartland straddled the great east-west routes that would later be called the Silk Road: the caravan tracks running from the Mediterranean through Mesopotamia, over the Zagros, across the Iranian plateau, and onward to Bactria, Sogdiana, and the markets of Han China. Whoever controlled Media and Mesopotamia controlled the tolls. Whoever controlled the tolls could pay the cavalry that held Media and Mesopotamia. Mithridates seems to have grasped this circular logic with unusual clarity.

His military revolution drew on two traditions that, until then, had rarely been fused effectively. From the steppe came the horse archer - light, fast, capable of loosing arrows at a gallop and melting away before heavy infantry could close. From the settled Iranian nobility came the cataphract, a lancer armored from helmet to horse's hoof in overlapping scale, built to shatter formations in a single shock. Mithridates-era Parthia perfected the combination. Archers harassed and exhausted; cataphracts delivered the killing blow. It was a system engineered for open country, and open country was exactly what lay between the Oxus and the Euphrates.

He also understood the importance of timing. Mithridates did not launch a grand war of conquest in a single campaign season. He picked his moments. When the Seleucid king Demetrius I Soter was distracted by rebellions in Syria and a usurper named Timarchus seized Media, Mithridates watched. When the Greco-Bactrian king Eucratides I turned his attention southward into India, Mithridates watched the eastern frontier too. The Arsacid court appears to have maintained an informational network - envoys, merchants, exiled noblemen - that told the king where his enemies were weakest.

His brother Phraates, who had preceded him briefly on the throne, had already begun probing westward into the Iranian plateau. Mithridates inherited not just a crown but a strategic direction. What was new was the scale of his ambition and the patience with which he pursued it. He seems to have decided, early in his reign, that Parthia's future lay not on the steppe but in the cities - in Ecbatana, in Seleucia, in the ancient Mesopotamian heartland where kings had ruled since the third millennium. That decision would reshape the map of Asia.

The Conquest of Media and Mesopotamia

The first great prize was Media. It was an obvious target and a difficult one. Media stretched across the northwestern Iranian plateau, its capital at Ecbatana - modern Hamadan - nestled in the Zagros highlands. It controlled the passes down to Mesopotamia and the roads east to Parthia itself. For the Seleucids, Media was the spine of their eastern empire. For Mithridates, it was both shield and gateway.

Around 148 or 147 BCE, Mithridates moved. The Seleucid governor of Media, Timarchus, had declared himself king some years earlier, exploiting the chaos in Antioch. His rebellion had been suppressed, but Media remained unsettled, its loyalties divided, its defenses patchy. Mithridates marched west through familiar country and took Ecbatana, seemingly without a prolonged siege. The summer capital of the old Achaemenid kings - where Darius had kept his treasure and Alexander had mourned Hephaestion - passed into Arsacid hands.

The symbolism was enormous. Ecbatana was not just a city; it was a memory. To hold it was to announce that the Arsacids were no longer bandit kings of the northeast but legitimate heirs to the old Iranian imperial tradition. Mithridates seems to have understood this instantly. He began minting coins in the city, and he made Ecbatana one of his royal residences, the cool mountain seat from which Parthian kings would later rule during the baking summers of the plain.

From Media the road ran downward, through the Zagros passes, into the lowlands of the Tigris and Euphrates. Mesopotamia was the wealthiest province on earth. Its cities - Seleucia on the Tigris, Babylon, Uruk - contained temples, banks, canals, and populations that counted in the hundreds of thousands. Its agricultural surplus, irrigated by two millennia of engineering, could fund armies indefinitely. Whoever held Mesopotamia was, by most definitions of the word, an empire.

In 141 BCE, Mithridates held it. The Parthian advance into Babylonia met surprisingly little organized resistance. The Seleucid grip had loosened; local elites - Babylonian priests, Greek merchants in Seleucia, Aramaic-speaking scribes - had less stake in Antioch than in their own continued prosperity. Mithridates offered stability. He did not sack the cities. He did not massacre the Greek populations. He issued coins proclaiming himself king and, crucially, had them struck in the established Seleucid style, with

Greek legends and familiar iconography. Continuity, not rupture, was the message.

Cuneiform astronomical diaries from Babylon - kept by temple scribes who recorded celestial events and political developments with equal diligence - mention the arrival of the Parthian king and his acceptance by the city. For the priests of Marduk, one foreign dynasty had simply replaced another. The offerings continued. The canals were maintained. Business went on.

The Seleucids did not, of course, accept the loss quietly. Demetrius II Nicator, the reigning king in Antioch, launched a counter-campaign into the east, hoping to rally the Iranian provinces against the new occupiers. He failed spectacularly. Parthian forces captured him in 138 BCE. Mithridates, rather than execute his royal prisoner, kept him in honorable confinement and eventually married him to a Parthian princess - the Seleucid king as Arsacid son-in-law, humiliated and co-opted in a single stroke.

A decade later, in 129 BCE, Demetrius's brother Antiochus VII would mount a final, determined attempt to reclaim the east. He too would die in the effort, his army annihilated on the Iranian plateau by Mithridates's successors. The pattern set in the 140s would hold. Mesopotamia, once lost, was lost for good.

Crowning in Seleucia: Claiming the Heritage of Kings

Of all the ceremonies Mithridates staged, none mattered more than the one at Seleucia in 141 BCE. The choice of city was itself a statement. Seleucia on the Tigris was the great Greek foundation of the East, built by Seleucus I a century and a half earlier to be the administrative anchor of his empire. Its population may have reached half a million. Its streets were laid out on the Hippodamian grid. Its law courts used Greek procedure. Its citizens voted, after a fashion, in civic assemblies modeled on those of Athens and Miletus. If any city symbolized the Seleucid project in Asia, it was Seleucia.

By holding an investiture ceremony there, Mithridates was not merely occupying the city. He was asserting that the Arsacid dynasty had inherited what the Seleucids had lost - not just the territory but the legitimacy, the relationship with the urban Greek world, the role of universal monarch. The ceremony appears to have followed Hellenistic conventions: proclamations, processions, the minting of commemorative tetradrachms bearing the king's diademed portrait.

Those coins repay close attention. The portraiture is strikingly Greek in technique - a three-quarters profile, a neatly trimmed beard, the royal diadem knotted behind the head. The reverse shows a seated archer, the Arsacid dynastic emblem, a nod to the horse-archer roots of the family. The legends are in Greek. And the title Mithridates chose was, for this moment, deliberately restrained: *BASILEUS MEGAS ARSAKES* - Great King Arsaces. He took his founder's name as a throne name, an Arsacid convention that every subsequent king would follow, and he adopted the Hellenistic superlative *Megas*.

The message was calibrated for a Greek audience. Mithridates was not a barbarian conqueror come to burn the library. He was a legitimate Hellenistic sovereign who happened to be of Iranian descent, a king in the tradition of Alexander and his successors, worthy of the loyalty that Seleucia's citizens had given to previous dynasties. He even added to his coinage the epithet *Philhellene* - friend of the Greeks. It was perhaps the shrewdest piece of imperial branding in the ancient world.

At the same time, in other contexts, Mithridates communicated differently. In the Iranian highlands, his court invoked the Achaemenid past - the memory of Cyrus, Darius, Xerxes. In Babylonia, he allowed himself to be addressed in the old Mesopotamian formulas, king of the lands, beloved of Marduk. In Parthia proper, he remained an Arsacid chieftain among chieftains, first among noble equals. The Parthian Empire would always be, in a sense, a federation of masks. Mithridates was its first great actor.

The Seleucia ceremony also served a practical purpose. It told the local elites
- Greek magistrates, Babylonian priests, Aramaic-speaking bureaucrats -
that they had a new patron who would protect their privileges in exchange
for loyalty. The contract was explicit. Cities would keep their institutions.
Temples would keep their lands. Merchants would keep their trade. In return,
the Arsacids would collect taxes and conduct the foreign policy of the realm.
It was a bargain the Seleucids had once offered and increasingly failed to
honor. Mithridates honored it, and the bargain held, with periodic tremors,
for nearly four centuries.

Eastern Expansion Toward Bactria

While Mithridates was crowning himself in Mesopotamia, trouble was
brewing a thousand miles to the east. The Greco-Bactrian kingdom, which
had ruled the lands beyond the Oxus since breaking from the Seleucids in
the mid-third century BCE, was entering its terminal crisis. Its king,
Eucratides I, had made himself formidable through a combination of ruthless
ambition and military skill, but his attention was pulled in multiple
directions. Indian campaigns to the south. Nomadic pressure from the north.
Dynastic rivals closer to home.

Mithridates saw his chance. Parthian forces pushed east across the plateau,
absorbing provinces that had drifted out of Bactrian control. The details of
these campaigns are frustratingly thin - the sources, mostly late and
fragmentary, give us outlines rather than battles - but the results are clear.
By the end of Mithridates's reign, Parthia controlled Aria, Margiana, and
parts of what is now western Afghanistan. The frontier had moved hundreds
of miles eastward.

The gains were more than territorial. They placed Parthia astride the Silk
Road at its most valuable pinch point, the corridor through which silk,
lacquer, jade, and bronze moved westward from Han China and through
which glass, wool, and silver moved east. Whoever held Margiana - with its

great oasis city of Merv - held the tolls on the most lucrative long-distance trade in the ancient world. Mithridates held Merv.

The eastern frontier also brought the Parthians into contact, and conflict, with the nomadic confederations of the Central Asian steppe. The Saka - Iranian-speaking horsemen related to the Scythians of the Pontic steppe - had been pressed southward by movements further north, themselves triggered by Han Chinese pressure on the Xiongnu. It was a domino effect spanning a continent. Around 140 BCE, Mithridates inflicted a significant defeat on Saka forces pushing into his new eastern provinces. The victory stabilized the frontier for a generation.

It would not last. The nomadic pressure was relentless, and later Arsacid kings - Phraates II and Artabanus I - would both die fighting the Saka. But in Mithridates's lifetime, the eastern frontier held. Cataphract cavalry combined with local fortifications proved sufficient, at least, to turn back the initial waves.

The Bactrian campaigns also introduced the Arsacids to a bewildering religious and cultural mix. In the cities of the east, Greek-speaking Hellenistic populations lived alongside Iranian Zoroastrians, Indian Buddhists, and local cults of great antiquity. Coins from the region show deities from four or five different pantheons sharing the same die-cutters. Parthia, already pluralistic, became more so. The empire Mithridates left to his heirs was an empire of many gods, many languages, many legal traditions - held together by cavalry, coin, and careful politics.

The Title King of Kings Returns

Somewhere in the last years of his reign - the precise date is disputed - Mithridates made his boldest claim. On certain coins, and possibly in formal proclamations, he adopted the title *Shahanshah*, King of Kings. It was not a title anyone had used seriously in Iran for nearly two hundred years.

The phrase carried specific historical weight. It was the title of Cyrus the Great, of Darius, of Xerxes - the Achaemenid emperors whose armies had once crossed into Greece and whose palaces at Persepolis and Susa still stood, half-ruined, on the Iranian plateau. Alexander had destroyed that empire, and his successors had avoided the title, preferring the Greek *Basileus*. To resurrect *Shahanshah* was to claim continuity not with the Hellenistic kings but with the Persian Great Kings they had replaced.

The political logic was sharp. Mithridates now ruled over many subordinate rulers - client kings in Armenia, Characene, Elymais, Persis, and beyond. Each of these had his own crown, his own capital, his own coinage. The Arsacid king was, quite literally, a king over kings. The title described reality. But it also made a claim about legitimacy: that reality had a precedent, that the Achaemenid order was being restored after two centuries of Greek interruption.

How seriously Mithridates pressed the claim is uncertain. His Greek-facing coinage continued to emphasize Hellenistic legitimacy and the epithet *Philhellene*. The Iranian-facing claim to Achaemenid inheritance was quieter, more selective, perhaps aimed at the Iranian nobility whose loyalty he needed most. Later Arsacids would embrace the title more openly. Under them, King of Kings became the standard formula of Parthian monarchy, and it would pass, eventually, to the Sasanians who overthrew them.

Mithridates died around 138 BCE, probably in his sixties. He had reigned for roughly three decades. He had taken a frontier kingdom and turned it into the dominant power between the Mediterranean and the Indus.

Key Figures and Events

Mithridates I (reigned c. 171-138 BCE) was the architect of Parthian greatness - soldier, diplomat, and image-maker in equal measure. His brother Phraates I had prepared the westward direction of Arsacid policy; Mithridates executed it at imperial scale. Timarchus, the Seleucid usurper in

Media, created the opening through which Parthia entered the plateau. Demetrius I Soter and his successors Demetrius II Nicator and Antiochus VII Sidetes represented the declining Seleucid attempt to hold the east, each in turn defeated or captured. Eucratides I of Bactria, fighting on too many fronts, was unable to prevent Parthian absorption of his western provinces.

The decisive moments are easily listed: the capture of Ecbatana around 148 or 147 BCE; the conquest of Babylonia and the Seleucia investiture in 141 BCE; the defeat of the Saka around 140 BCE; the capture of Demetrius II in 138 BCE. Within roughly a decade, the regional order of western Asia was remade.

Analysis

Why did Mithridates succeed where others failed? Partly it was timing - the Seleucid collapse and the Bactrian crisis happened to overlap in the 140s BCE, and he was ready to exploit both. Partly it was military - the cataphract-and-archer combination gave Parthian armies a flexibility that heavy Hellenistic phalanxes could not match on the open plateau. But most of all it was political intelligence. Mithridates understood that a durable empire needed local elites on its side, not underfoot. He left Greek cities their institutions, Babylonian temples their revenues, Iranian nobles their estates. He asked for taxes, soldiers, and loyalty; he offered protection, continuity, and prestige. The bargain worked.

His deeper significance lies in what he made possible. By placing Parthia astride the trade routes from Syria to Bactria, he created the conditions for the great east-west commerce of the Silk Road era. By resurrecting the title of King of Kings, he re-Iranized the political imagination of western Asia after two centuries of Greek domination. By demonstrating that an Iranian dynasty could rule pluralistically over Greeks, Babylonians, Arameans, and nomads alike, he established a template that would outlast him by four hundred years and influence the Sasanian and even the early Islamic caliphates.

Quick Summary

- Mithridates I (r. c. 171-138 BCE) transformed Parthia from a regional kingdom into an empire stretching from the Euphrates to the edge of India.
- He exploited Seleucid internal chaos and Greco-Bactrian distraction to conquer Media (c. 148/147 BCE), capturing the strategic capital of Ecbatana.
- In 141 BCE he took Babylonia and staged a Hellenistic-style investiture at Seleucia on the Tigris, signaling continuity with Greek urban institutions.
- His coinage combined Greek portraiture, the epithet *Philhellene*, and eventually the revived Achaemenid title King of Kings.
- Parthian forces defeated the Saka around 140 BCE, temporarily stabilizing the eastern frontier.
- Seleucid king Demetrius II Nicator was captured in 138 BCE and held as an honored prisoner, then married to a Parthian princess.
- Mithridates pioneered a pluralist imperial model - multiple masks for multiple audiences - that would sustain Parthian rule for centuries.
- His conquests placed Parthia at the heart of the emerging Silk Road trade network linking Rome and Han China.

When he was laid to rest, probably in one of the royal tombs near Nisa, the old Parthian capital in what is now Turkmenistan, Mithridates left a state that had outgrown its origins. The horse-archers of the steppe now collected taxes in Aramaic and minted tetradrachms in Greek. Their king had been crowned in a city named for Alexander's general and had claimed the title of Cyrus. The Arsacid synthesis - Iranian at the core, Hellenistic on the surface,

Mesopotamian in its wealth, nomadic in its military bones - was his creation. Rome, still busy digesting Carthage, barely noticed. Within a century, Roman legions would learn, at terrible cost, exactly what Mithridates had built.

Mithridates left his heirs a state that stretched from the Euphrates to the edge of India, but a map is not a government. An empire assembled that quickly, out of Greek cities, Iranian nobles, Mesopotamian scribes, and steppe cavalry, should by every reasonable expectation have fallen apart within a generation. It did not. For nearly five centuries it held together through an arrangement that looked, to Roman eyes, almost improvised - a patchwork of vassal kings, noble houses, and tolerated cities. How that machinery actually worked is the puzzle worth examining next.

Chapter 3:

The Machinery of a Decentralized Empire

When a Parthian king rode to war, he did not command a unified state. He summoned it - one noble house, one vassal king, one Greek city at a time.

This is the puzzle at the heart of Parthian success. For nearly five centuries the Arsacid dynasty ruled an empire stretching from the Euphrates to the Hindu Kush, fending off Rome in the west and steppe raiders in the east. Yet compared with the Roman state machine - its legions, censors, and provincial governors reporting to a single capital - the Parthian system looks almost improvised. Local kings kept their crowns. Noble families fielded private armies. Greek cities minted their own coins and ran their own councils. The king at Ctesiphon took tribute and soldiers, but rarely tried to dissolve the layered loyalties beneath him. Historians once read this as weakness: a half-built empire, always on the verge of fracture. Seen from another angle, it was the secret of its longevity. A looser structure bent where a rigid one would have snapped. It absorbed defeats - three separate Roman captures of the capital itself - and still outlasted many of the regimes that assaulted it. To understand the Parthians, you have to understand how power actually moved through their world.

The King of Kings and His Limits

The Arsacid monarch called himself *shahanshah* - King of Kings. The title was not bluster. It was an accurate description of the job.

Unlike a Roman emperor, who in theory answered to no one and ruled citizens directly, the Parthian sovereign ruled mostly through other rulers. Beneath him sat crowned kings of Armenia, Characene, Elymais, Adiabene, Osroene, and more. Beside him stood the heads of ancient noble houses whose lands and retainers predated the Arsacids themselves. The king's personal authority was real, but it was exercised across a political terrain of other people's crowns.

The dynasty grew into this role gradually. Arsaces I, the semi-legendary founder who carved out a foothold in the northeast around the mid-third century BCE, was at first little more than a successful chieftain. It took generations before his heirs could style themselves overlords of kings. Mithradates I, who reigned from 171 to 138 BCE, was the man who made the title mean something. His armies swept across the Iranian Plateau and down into the Tigris-Euphrates valley, and for the first time the Arsacid court presided over a genuinely imperial patchwork. Mithridates II, ruling from 123 to 88 BCE, took the next step: he reduced neighboring kingdoms - Armenia among them, where he installed his own son - to the status of vassals. After him, the phrase *King of Kings* on coinage was no longer aspirational.

Yet the limits were severe, and every Arsacid knew it. Succession was never cleanly hereditary. A council of nobles and senior royal relatives had a voice - sometimes a decisive voice - in choosing the next king. Candidates from the Arsacid line could be elevated or toppled depending on how the great houses read the political weather. Civil wars between rival claimants were frequent, and an unpopular king could find himself abandoned mid-campaign by the very magnates who had crowned him.

The king's direct writ, in practical terms, ran strongest on his own crown lands, in his treasury, and in the royal guard. Beyond that, power was negotiated. He could call upon the cavalry of the noble houses, but he could not disband them. He could appoint officials, but many positions were hereditary in particular families. He could demand tribute from vassal kings, but he could not easily depose them without a military campaign that might cost more than it yielded.

This is why so much Parthian politics looks, from the outside, like aristocratic theater. Royal hunts, ceremonial banquets, the elaborate giving and receiving of gifts, the investiture of client kings with diadems - these were not decoration. They were the working mechanisms by which a king without a bureaucratic state made his authority felt. Pageantry was governance. When a Roman envoy complained of Parthian ostentation, he was misreading what he saw. The ceremony *was* the state.

The weakness of the model showed whenever the center stumbled. Roman armies captured Ctesiphon in 116, 165, and 198 CE. Each time the dynasty survived - but each time it survived because the empire was not concentrated in one city. Power had somewhere else to live.

The Seven Great Houses

Where it lived, above all, was in the halls of the great noble clans. Later Iranian tradition remembers seven of them - the Suren, the Karen, the Mihran, the Spandiyadh, and others whose names survive only in fragments. The number seven may be a neat tradition rather than a hard count, but the reality it reflects is solid: a small number of immensely powerful aristocratic houses dominated the Arsacid order from beginning to end.

These families were not creations of the dynasty. Several predated it, rooted in the Iranian nobility of the Achaemenid and Seleucid periods. Their estates, often vast, sprawled across regions like Media, Parthia proper, and the northeast. Their private retinues of armored cavalry - the famed *cataphracts* - formed the striking arm of any Parthian army. When a king rode to war against Rome, he did so at the head of a coalition force, and the heaviest cavalry in that force answered first to a family banner and only second to his.

The Suren are the clan history remembers best, because of one man. In 53 BCE, at Carrhae in the deserts of northern Mesopotamia, a Surenid general - known to Roman sources simply as Surena - annihilated the legions of Marcus Licinius Crassus. He did it with roughly ten thousand horsemen, most of them his own household troops. He was not yet thirty. The victory was one of the most catastrophic defeats Rome had suffered in a generation, and it was won not by the Arsacid king in person but by a noble acting under his banner.

What happened next is instructive. King Orodes II, rather than rewarding the architect of his greatest triumph, had Surena executed. Whether from jealousy, fear, or cold political calculation hardly matters. The episode captures the central tension of the Parthian system in a single gesture. The great houses won the empire's wars. They also terrified its kings.

Certain offices at court were reportedly hereditary - the Suren, by tradition, placed the crown on a new king's head at his coronation. Other families held the right to command particular wings of the army, or to govern particular regions. These were not favors granted; they were ancestral claims that a king confirmed because he could not revoke them.

The practical effect was a permanent power-sharing arrangement. An able king who cultivated his magnates could mobilize extraordinary force. A weak or tactless one faced a different threat from what a Roman emperor faced in a bad year. A Roman was threatened by his own generals and bodyguards. A Parthian king was threatened by independent aristocrats with independent armies, independent estates, and independent genealogies often older than his own.

Civil wars erupted when those balances failed. Rival Arsacid princes could almost always find a great house willing to back them - sometimes because of marriage alliances, sometimes because of local rivalries, sometimes because a faction among the nobles simply preferred a weaker candidate they could manage. The recurrence of these struggles has often been read as proof of Parthian dysfunction. It is better read as proof of what the Arsacid state actually was: a coalition, permanently renegotiated, of families who ruled Iran together.

When Ardašir, a minor Persian prince, finally overthrew the last Arsacid, Artabanus IV, in 224 CE, he did not simply defeat a king. He assembled his own coalition of nobles who had concluded that the Arsacid compact had run its course. The houses that had made the dynasty unmade it.

Vassal Kingdoms: Elymais, Characene, Adiabene, Osroene

Beyond the noble estates of the Iranian heartland lay a second tier of power: the vassal kingdoms. These were real states, with their own kings, their own coinage, their own dynastic lines, their own religions. They paid tribute to Ctesiphon and supplied troops when summoned. Otherwise, they governed themselves.

Elymais lay in the rugged country of what is now southwestern Iran, the old land of Elam. Its kings, operating from hill fortresses and the ancient sanctuary at Susa's hinterland, minted coins bearing their own portraits and titles well into the second century CE. Their realm was mountainous and defensible, and Arsacid armies periodically had to remind them which way tribute flowed. When the Seleucid king Antiochus III had tried to plunder an Elymaean temple in 187 BCE, he was killed in the attempt - a warning the Parthians noted. Light control, regular tribute, and a wary respect for local sanctuaries proved the more durable policy.

At the head of the Persian Gulf sat Characene, a kingdom built around the port city of Charax Spasinou. Its wealth came from the sea. Ships from India docked at its wharves; caravans from Arabia arrived at its gates; and the goods then moved up the Tigris and Euphrates to the markets of Mesopotamia. Characene paid the Arsacids in coin, duties, and access to the trade that flowed through its harbors. In return, its kings enjoyed a latitude that looked, at moments, almost like independence. Their coinage ran continuously for centuries. When a Parthian king needed silver, Characene's mints were among his quieter but most valuable assets.

North of Mesopotamia, in the broken country between the Tigris and the Zagros foothills, lay Adiabene. Its capital was Arbela - modern Erbil, one of the oldest continuously inhabited cities in the world. Adiabene's royal house is best remembered for a remarkable religious episode: in the first century CE, Queen Helena and her son King Izates converted to Judaism. Helena traveled to Jerusalem, funded famine relief, and was buried in a monumental tomb still identifiable there. The conversion tells us something important about the latitude Parthian vassals enjoyed. A subordinate king could adopt a new religion, patronize foreign holy cities, and involve his kingdom in the affairs of Roman-ruled Judea - all without apparent objection from his overlord at Ctesiphon. What mattered was loyalty and tribute, not theological uniformity.

Osroene, centered on Edessa in what is now southeastern Turkey, was the westernmost of the significant vassals and thus the most exposed. It sat directly in the path of every Roman campaign east. Its Abgarid dynasty became skilled at a delicate diplomatic balance: sending troops to Parthian musters, negotiating with Roman generals, opening the gates when armies were close and shutting them when they retreated. Osroene, too, would become famous for religious change - early tradition holds that Edessa was among the first cities to adopt Christianity, with its royal house reportedly converting in the early third century. Like Adiabene, it shows how much spiritual independence the Arsacid framework permitted.

What tied these kingdoms to the empire was not a uniform administrative code. It was a bundle of obligations, renewed at each succession: recognition of the King of Kings, military service when summoned, payment of tribute, and the acceptance - at least in principle - that the Arsacid court could intervene in disputed successions. In exchange, local dynasties kept their thrones, their gods, their languages, and their local privileges. When Romans stormed through northern Mesopotamia, these vassal kingdoms bent, submitted, and then quietly reasserted themselves once the legions withdrew. They were shock absorbers. Empires designed for rigidity tend to break; the Arsacid empire was designed to flex.

Greek Cities Under Arsacid Rule

There was a third layer, and it spoke Greek. When the Parthians took Mesopotamia from the Seleucids in the second century BCE, they inherited a constellation of Greek and Greek-style cities: Seleucia-on-the-Tigris, the grandest of them, along with Susa, Dura-Europos, and many lesser foundations. These were not provincial towns. Seleucia alone may have held six hundred thousand inhabitants at its height, rivaling any city in the Mediterranean world.

The Arsacid solution to this inherited Hellenism was pragmatic. They did not dismantle it. Instead, they adopted it where it suited them and left it largely alone where it did not. Their early coins were struck in Greek, with Greek titles, often bearing the legend *philhellene* - friend of the Greeks. Their court employed Greek-speaking officials and entertained Greek performers. Plutarch tells us that when the head of the defeated Crassus was delivered to the Parthian king's banquet, a troupe of actors was midway through a performance of Euripides' *Bacchae* - a detail that perfectly captures the cultural amphibiousness of the Arsacid court.

Greek cities were allowed to keep their internal institutions. Seleucia retained its council, its assembly, its elected magistrates. It minted its own bronze coinage and ran its own courts for most local matters. A royal representative oversaw the city's relationship with the crown and collected taxes, but he did not replace the civic machinery. When Seleucia rebelled against Arsacid authority in the first century CE, the revolt took seven years to suppress - evidence that this was a city with real institutional muscle, not a puppet.

Dura-Europos on the Euphrates offers an unusually vivid picture because its ruins were so well preserved. Archaeologists have recovered papyri, parchments, graffiti, and temple reliefs that show a town functioning in Greek administrative forms, praying to gods Greek, Iranian, and Semitic, and writing in several languages at once. A Parthian garrison watched over it. A Greek-descended elite ran it. Caravan merchants from across the empire transacted in it. This was the texture of Parthian urbanism: overlapping identities, coexisting in a city the central authority was content to tax rather than transform.

Over the long run, the balance shifted. By the first century CE, Parthian kings began to drop the *philhellene* legend from their coins. Aramaic and Middle Iranian scripts crept onto royal inscriptions. The court's Iranian identity grew more assertive. But the Greek cities were never crushed - they simply became one thread in a more openly multicultural fabric. The willingness to let Seleucia be Seleucia, while demanding only taxes and loyalty, was a political choice that spared the Arsacids a century of rebellion they had no desire to fight.

Taxation, Tribute, and the Royal Roads

What did the king actually collect, and how did he collect it? The honest answer is that we know less than we would like. Parthian archives have not survived. What evidence we have comes from coins, scattered inscriptions, Greek and Roman observers, and a handful of documents from frontier cities like Dura-Europos.

Revenue came in three main streams. First, tribute from vassal kingdoms - fixed payments, probably negotiated at each royal accession, paid in silver and in kind. Second, direct taxes from the king's own crown lands and from cities under direct Arsacid administration. Third, customs duties on the caravan trade that crossed the empire from east to west and north to south.

That third stream may have been the most lucrative. The Parthians sat astride the land routes linking Han China, Central Asia, India, and the Mediterranean. Silk, spices, glass, and silver flowed across their territory, and every significant crossing, every major city, every port collected its share. Roman writers complained bitterly about the gold draining east to pay for eastern luxuries. A good deal of that gold stopped at Parthian tollhouses before it ever reached China.

The infrastructure that made this work was partly inherited. The Achaemenid Royal Road, built nearly five centuries earlier, still ran from the Aegean coast deep into Iran, and the Seleucids had maintained and extended it. The Parthians used it, manned its way stations, and kept its bridges. Mounted couriers could carry royal messages across vast distances in days rather than weeks. Caravans paid the duties that kept the system funded.

Administration of all this was, by Roman standards, minimal. There was no census bureaucracy on the scale of imperial Rome's, no professional class of provincial governors rotated from the capital. Tax collection was often farmed out - to local officials, to city magistrates, to vassal kings who deducted a share before remitting the rest. It was a light hand, easily evaded in bad times, but cheap to maintain in good ones. That was rather the point.

Key Figures & Events

The dynasty's decentralized machinery took shape around a handful of decisive moments and personalities. Arsaces I, in the mid-third century BCE, established the foundational compact with the Iranian nobility that would define the regime for five hundred years. Mithradates I, reigning 171-138 BCE, conquered the territories that turned a kingdom into an empire, bringing Mesopotamia and its Greek cities under Arsacid rule. Mithridates II, ruling 123-88 BCE, codified the vassal system, reducing Armenia and other neighboring realms to tributary status and installing his own relatives on their thrones. Surena's victory at Carrhae in 53 BCE demonstrated both the power of the great houses and the paranoia it bred in kings. Roman captures of Ctesiphon in 116, 165, and 198 CE tested the decentralized model to its limits and proved it could survive losses that would have destroyed a more centralized state. Finally, Ardašir's overthrow of Artabanus IV in 224 CE ended the Arsacid dynasty - accomplished, tellingly, by the same method the Arsacids themselves had relied on: a coalition of nobles choosing a new king.

Analysis

Why did this system work for so long, and why did it eventually fail? It worked because it matched the terrain it governed. Iran and Mesopotamia were not a single flat political surface. They were mountains and river valleys, steppe and desert, Greek cities and Semitic merchant towns and Iranian noble estates, all with long histories and deep local loyalties. A centralized Roman-style state would have required a staggering bureaucratic effort to impose uniformity on such diversity - and would likely have provoked precisely the kind of unified resistance that the Arsacid compromise avoided.

The decentralized model also had strategic virtues. When Rome struck, it could take the capital, but it could not take the empire. Vassal kings submitted, waited, and reemerged. Noble houses retreated to their estates and raised fresh cavalry. The political center was not a point on the map; it was a network of agreements, and networks are famously hard to destroy.

But the same features that provided resilience set a ceiling on power. A king who needed consent could not move as decisively as one who did not. Civil wars between Arsacid claimants recurred because the great houses could always find a candidate to back, and because no king could ever fully pacify his own nobility. By the late second and early third centuries CE, after generations of Roman invasions and internal succession struggles, the compact was fraying. Ardašir did not invent a new form of state so much as persuade enough of the old stakeholders that a tighter, more Persianized, more centralized regime would serve them better. The Sasanian Empire that followed would be more autocratic, more bureaucratic, and more religiously uniform. It would also, eventually, break more suddenly than its predecessor. That is the trade-off running through the whole history of the ancient Near East: rigidity buys intensity at the cost of resilience, and flexibility buys endurance at the cost of command.

Quick Summary

- The Parthian Empire was not a centralized state but a layered coalition of the King of Kings, great noble houses, vassal kingdoms, and semi-autonomous Greek cities.
- The Arsacid monarch's authority was real but limited by noble councils, hereditary offices, and the military power of independent aristocratic clans.
- Seven great houses - the Suren, Karen, Mihran, and others - provided the empire's heavy cavalry and periodically threatened its kings, as the career and execution of Surena after Carrhae (53 BCE) illustrates.
- Vassal kingdoms such as Elymais, Characene, Adiabene, and Osroene kept their own dynasties, coinage, and religions in exchange for tribute and military service.
- Greek cities like Seleucia-on-the-Tigris and Dura-Europos retained their civic institutions; early Arsacid kings styled themselves *philhellene* on their coins.
- Revenue flowed from tribute, crown-land taxes, and - crucially - customs duties on the Silk Road trade traversing the empire.
- The decentralized structure allowed the empire to survive multiple Roman captures of Ctesiphon but left it vulnerable to internal coalitions, which ultimately brought Ardašir to power in 224 CE.

The Parthian machinery looks, at first glance, like a state that never quite became one. That impression is misleading. It was a state built to do specific things: hold a vast, diverse territory together without the administrative apparatus Rome possessed, and survive catastrophic military defeats without collapsing. For nearly five centuries it did both. When it finally fell, it fell not to foreign conquest but to its own internal logic - the same coalition-making that had crowned Arsacid kings for generations chose, at last, to crown someone else. The empire that replaced it would borrow much of its inheritance. But the particular genius of the Arsacid compromise - the willingness to rule lightly, to tolerate difference, to govern through other rulers rather than around them - would not be seen again in Iran for a very long time.

A decentralized empire held together by coalition and compromise still had to defend itself, and in the ancient world defense meant armies. The Arsacid system of vassal kings and noble houses was not only a way of collecting taxes. It was a way of raising cavalry. Each great house brought its own armored lancers and horse-archers to the king's summons, and the same coalition logic that governed the empire in peace delivered it to the battlefield in war. The result was a way of fighting unlike anything Rome had faced before.

Chapter 4:

Horsemen and Cataphracts: The Parthian Way of War

On a blistering afternoon in June of 53 BCE, somewhere on the dust plains near the town of Carrhae, a Roman army of roughly forty thousand men discovered that arrows could fall for hours without stopping. They had expected a brief skirmish. They got an execution.

The Parthians did something that should not, by the logic of Mediterranean warfare, have worked. They fielded no heavy infantry - no phalanx, no legions, no sword-and-shield line to anchor a battlefield. Their army was built on two kinds of horsemen and almost nothing else: the light horse archer, who struck from a distance and vanished before a counterblow could land, and the cataphract, an armored rider on an armored horse who shattered formations the archers had softened. Between them, these two arms produced one of the most effective military systems of the ancient world. That system humbled Crassus at Carrhae, frustrated Mark Antony a generation later, and kept Roman ambitions east of the Euphrates permanently uncertain for nearly three centuries. To understand how a small feudal confederation of Iranian nobles could stand against the machine of Rome, you have to understand the horse, the bow, and the social order that put them together.

The Horse Archer and the Composite Bow

The horse archer was not a Parthian invention. He was a steppe inheritance, a figure already ancient by the time the Parni rode south into Iran in the third century BCE. What the Parthians did was take a nomadic way of fighting and wire it into the bones of an imperial army.

Begin with the weapon. The Parthian bow was a composite bow - a laminated construction of wood, horn, and sinew glued in layers and bent against its natural curvature. Dried for months, sometimes years, it stored extraordinary energy in a short frame. A stave of plain wood of comparable draw weight would have been too long to shoot from horseback. The composite bow could be drawn to the ear by a rider at full gallop, and the arrow it sent had the punch to pierce a mail shirt at close range and wound through a scutum at longer ones. Roman sources at Carrhae record arrows pinning hands to shields and feet to the ground.

Next, the horse. The Parthian riding horse was a descendant of steppe breeds crossed with the larger Nisaean stock of the Iranian plateau - quick, tough, and accustomed to hard ground and sparse water. A horse archer often led one or more remounts, switching animals to keep his unit fresh across a day of skirmishing. This, too, was a steppe habit transplanted into imperial logistics.

Then the skill. A horse archer had to do three things at once: guide a moving animal with his knees, draw a heavy bow against the shock of the gallop, and loose with accuracy at a target that was itself likely moving. Parthian boys of the nobility and of the client tribes practiced this from early childhood. The Greek historian Justin, summarizing Pompeius Trogus, noted that Parthians spent their youth almost entirely on horseback, hunting and shooting, and that a Parthian on foot was considered half a man.

From this training came the signature trick - the one that entered every European language that borrowed a word from the east: the Parthian shot. A rider would gallop directly away from the enemy, feigning flight, then twist at the waist and shoot backward over his horse's rump. The maneuver required a rare combination of seat, grip, and timing, and it was devastating against pursuers who thought the fight was over. A cavalryman chasing a "fleeing" Parthian would find himself meeting an arrow between the eyes of his own horse.

What mattered tactically was the cumulative effect. A horse-archer unit did not need to close. It could orbit an enemy formation at distance, loose volleys, wheel away when threatened, and return. Against a static infantry line standing in the heat, unable to pursue effectively, this produced a slow, grinding attrition: men pierced, horses crippled, shields rendered useless by the weight of embedded shafts, water and nerves dwindling by the hour.

Carrhae is the canonical demonstration. Crassus's legionaries locked shields in the *testudo* to ward off the rain of arrows, only to discover that the Parthians had brought a baggage train of camels loaded with spare arrows. The barrage did not stop. When Roman cavalry sallied out to drive the archers off, they were drawn away from the main body and cut down. By evening, some twenty thousand Romans were dead and another ten thousand prisoners. Crassus himself was killed during negotiations the next day. The man who had once been the richest in Rome ended, according to a later and probably apocryphal tale, with molten gold poured down his throat.

The Cataphract: Ancient Armor in Motion

The horse archer alone could not take a city, hold a pass, or break a disciplined line that refused to come apart. For that, the Parthians had the cataphract.

The word comes from the Greek *kataphraktos*, meaning "fully armored" or "covered over." A Parthian noble in full cataphract equipment wore a helmet of riveted iron, a long coat of scale or mail reaching below the knees, separate sleeves or manicae of articulated plates for the arms, and greaves for the shins. His horse wore a caparison of bronze or iron scales, sometimes reinforced with a chamfron over the face. Plutarch, describing the Parthian host at Carrhae, marveled at how the armor shone "like flashes of flame."

The primary weapon was not the bow but the *kontos* - a two-handed lance, four meters long or more, couched along the flank of the charging horse. Held in both hands, it left no hand free for a shield; the armor was the shield. A secondary sword or mace hung at the hip for the close work after a charge dissolved into melee.

The purpose of the cataphract was shock. A wedge of them at the canter was a moving wall of metal, and a line of infantry that had been peppered for hours by arrows - whose front ranks were wounded and whose shields were studded with shafts - could break at the sight of that wall coming on. If the wedge struck home, the kontos would punch through shield and mail and sometimes through two men at once. The mass of the armored horse did the rest.

Cataphracts were not cheap. A full panoply of scale armor for horse and rider represented the accumulated resources of a small estate. Each cataphract was effectively a self-financing noble - a landed warrior who owed the king armed service in exchange for his holding, and who brought his own equipment, his own grooms, and often a train of light horsemen drawn from his retainers. This is why the Parthian heavy cavalry was always, in absolute numbers, small. At Carrhae, Surena probably fielded a thousand cataphracts among something like ten thousand total horsemen. A thousand was enough, because the archers had already done most of the work.

The combination was the point. Horse archers could not close; cataphracts could not sustain a long engagement, given the exhaustion of carrying so much weight in the heat. One arm wore an enemy down; the other broke him. Neither alone was decisive. Together, they were something new in the ancient Near East - or rather, something very old, the steppe way of war, refined and scaled up into an imperial system.

This model would outlast the Parthians themselves. The Sasanians inherited it, refined it further, and passed it on to the Byzantines, who built their own *kataphraktoi* around the same logic. The armored lancer galloping out of an

Iranian plain would, through long genealogies of imitation, become the knight of medieval Europe.

Tactics, Logistics, and the Feigned Retreat

Parthian tactics read, at first glance, like a catalogue of tricks: the feigned retreat, the encirclement, the ambush, the Parthian shot. In practice, they were variations on a single idea. The Parthian commander wanted to keep his enemy moving, exposed, and frustrated, while his own forces remained mobile, supplied, and patient.

The feigned retreat was the most famous ploy. A unit of horse archers would engage, break contact, and flee - convincingly, even desperately. A pursuing force, assuming the skirmish was over, would follow. The flight would lead them across open country, away from their supports, until they ran into a screen of fresh archers, or cataphracts waiting in dead ground, or simply into terrain where the "fleeing" Parthians turned around and resumed shooting. Many commanders in antiquity knew the trick in the abstract. Very few could resist it in the moment, because it rewarded exactly the aggressive instincts that made a Roman or Macedonian officer effective against other opponents.

At Carrhae, the trick worked twice in a single day. Publius Crassus, the son of the Roman general, led a mixed force of Gallic cavalry and auxiliaries out after a retreating Parthian wing. He was drawn a mile or more from the main body, surrounded, and annihilated. His head was brought back to the legions on the point of a lance. The psychological effect on Crassus senior, and on the men who saw it, was precisely the one Surena had calculated.

Behind these tactics lay logistics that Roman observers badly underestimated. Parthian armies moved with strings of remounts, herds of baggage camels, and pre-positioned caches of arrows. Surena's innovation at Carrhae - the camel train of spare shafts - was less a flash of genius than an application of standard steppe practice to a formal battle. A Roman army counted arrows in the quivers of its auxiliaries. A Parthian army counted them by the cartload.

Terrain shaped everything. Parthian forces fought best on open ground where cavalry could wheel and where visibility was long. They avoided pitched battle in broken country, in forests, and above all in the confined spaces where Roman infantry excelled. Their strategic instinct was to lure invaders deep into the Mesopotamian plain in summer, where heat, dust, and distance from supply did much of the work before the first arrow flew. When Roman armies kept to the high country of Armenia or the narrow valleys of the Zagros, they did better. When they marched onto the flat, they risked Carrhae.

The Parthian commander also understood something that escaped many of his enemies: that destroying an army and winning a war were not the same thing. Parthian strategy aimed less at conquest than at exhausting an invader's will. A Roman force that crossed the Euphrates could be bled, harassed, and starved until it turned back. The border stayed where it had been. This patience, as much as any tactical flourish, is what kept Rome out of Iran.

Recruitment from the Noble Levies

A question has been lurking behind all of this. Where did these soldiers come from? The Parthian Empire had no permanent standing army in the Roman sense - no legions drawing a state salary, no annual enlistment. How did it put tens of thousands of horsemen in the field?

The army was, in effect, the aristocracy on horseback. Parthian society was organized around a handful of great noble houses - the Suren, the Karen, the Mihran, and others - each with vast estates, their own fortresses, and their own followings of lesser nobles and armed retainers. Beneath the great houses stood a broader class of landed gentry, the *azatan*, or "free ones," who held smaller estates on terms that bound them to military service.

Beneath them stood the peasants and clients who worked the land and, when called, rode out as the light horse archers of their lord's contingent.

When the king summoned the host, he was not raising troops in the modern sense. He was activating a web of obligations. The head of each noble house was expected to appear with a contingent proportionate to his lands - so many cataphracts from among his kin and senior retainers, so many mounted archers from his azatan and their followers. Surena, the general who won Carrhae, was a young nobleman of the Suren house. He brought, according to Plutarch, ten thousand horsemen - essentially his own family's private army - to reinforce the king's forces. That a single noble could put ten thousand cavalry in the field gives a sense of the scale at which this system operated.

This arrangement had enormous strengths. It was cheap for the crown, which did not have to feed and pay a standing force in peacetime. It produced warriors of superb quality, trained from childhood in riding and shooting as part of their social identity. And it meshed neatly with the decentralized structure of the empire, in which great nobles governed provinces as semi-independent vassals.

The weaknesses were equally structural. A king whose military depended on noble levies was a king who could not easily fight his own nobles. Parthian civil wars, of which there were many, often turned on which faction of the great houses backed which claimant. The army could not stay in the field indefinitely, because the men in it had estates and harvests to attend to. Long campaigns, sieges lasting years, garrisons in distant provinces - these were difficult, sometimes impossible, to sustain. Rome could keep a legion in Syria for a generation. Parthia could not keep a noble levy there for a summer.

Strengths, Weaknesses, and Siege Warfare

On open ground, in summer, against an army that had to be supplied from a distance, the combined arms of horse archer and cataphract were nearly unbeatable. Mobility gave the Parthians the initiative: they chose when to engage and when to disengage. Firepower at range exhausted enemies who could not reply in kind. The cataphract charge provided decisive shock when the moment came. And the whole system was built on a warrior class for whom fighting from horseback was not a profession but a birthright.

Without infantry, however, Parthian armies struggled in any environment that neutralized cavalry: mountains, forests, marshes, narrow valleys, urban streets. They could not easily hold ground. A Parthian force could cover a battlefield but not occupy it in the Roman sense - building a camp, digging ditches, and staying put. This made pursuit of a broken enemy efficient and garrison duty nearly impossible.

Siege warfare exposed the gap most starkly. Taking a walled city required engineering - towers, rams, mines, mantlets - and the patient infantry work of sappers, pioneers, and assault troops. The Parthians had little of this. They could blockade a city and starve it out, which required time they rarely had. They could sometimes borrow Greek or Mesopotamian engineers from their subject cities, but the technology never became native in the way it did for Rome. When Parthian armies took fortified places, it was usually because the defenders surrendered, defected, or were betrayed from within.

This weakness shaped the geography of the long Roman-Parthian frontier. Rome could take fortresses. Parthia could take armies. The result was a strange equilibrium in which Roman emperors from Trajan to Septimius Severus could march into Mesopotamia, storm cities like Ctesiphon, and then find themselves unable to hold the countryside or supply their lines. They would withdraw, and the Parthians would flow back across the plain.

Neither side could deliver a finishing blow. The frontier moved, but it did not break.

There was one other vulnerability, harder to see but no less important. The reliance on cavalry meant a reliance on horses, and horses needed pasture. A Parthian army in the field in late summer, after the grasses had burned out, was an army thinning by the day. Campaigns were seasonal, and seasons could be turned against a Parthian commander by an enemy willing to wait. Ventidius, a Roman general, learned this in 39-38 BCE, luring Parthian cavalry onto terrain where their tactics failed and winning the only clear Roman victories of the first century of the rivalry.

Key Figures and Events

Surena stands out as the strategist who made the system sing. A young nobleman - probably in his early thirties at Carrhae - he combined the resources of his house with the imagination to bring spare-arrow camels to a battle no one expected to last so long. King Orodes II, meanwhile, was campaigning elsewhere, in Armenia. Surena won the war for him. Orodes, characteristic of the tensions in Parthian politics, had Surena executed shortly afterward. A general that successful was a danger to his king.

Marcus Licinius Crassus, the loser at Carrhae, was a figure of enormous Roman prestige - the third member of the First Triumvirate with Caesar and Pompey, and by some measures the wealthiest private citizen in Roman history. His eastern campaign was driven less by strategic necessity than by personal ambition, a bid for military glory to match his partners. He crossed the Euphrates with seven legions and found a kind of warfare Roman training had not prepared him for. His death, and that of his son Publius, shocked Rome. The memory of Carrhae, and of the legionary standards lost there, haunted Roman politics for a generation, until Augustus negotiated their return in 20 BCE and celebrated it as if it were a victory.

Analysis

What Carrhae and the campaigns that followed really demonstrated was that there was more than one way to organize violence at scale in the ancient world. Rome's answer was heavy infantry, engineering, and a professional standing army funded by taxation. Parthia's answer was mobile cavalry, noble levies, and a feudal military aristocracy funded by land. These were not primitive versus advanced systems. They were different solutions to different problems, on different ground, against different enemies.

The Parthian system worked because it matched its geography and its society. The Iranian plateau and the Mesopotamian plain reward cavalry. The decentralized structure of the empire made a feudal levy natural. The steppe inheritance of the Parni provided the tactical vocabulary. When Roman armies brought their system onto Parthian ground, it failed more often than it succeeded. When Parthian armies tried to operate in Roman terrain - hilly Anatolia, fortified Syrian cities - they failed in turn. Each empire was most dangerous on its own kind of land, and the frontier between them marked, roughly, the boundary between those kinds of land.

Military effectiveness in antiquity was never a matter of pure tactics. It was a matter of fit - between weapons, men, society, and ground. The Parthians had fit.

Quick Summary

- The Parthian army had almost no heavy infantry, relying instead on light horse archers and heavily armored cataphracts.
- The composite bow and lifelong training from childhood made Parthian horse archers among the most effective missile troops of the ancient world.

- Cataphracts - armored riders on armored horses, wielding the long kontos lance - delivered the shock that followed the archers' attrition.
- The "Parthian shot," fired backward at full gallop, made feigned retreats deadly and entered European languages as a proverb.
- At Carrhae in 53 BCE, the general Surena used these combined tactics to destroy a Roman army of seven legions under Crassus.
- The army was recruited through noble levies, with great houses like the Suren bringing contingents of kin and retainers - cheap for the crown, but politically unstable.
- Parthian weaknesses included poor siege capability, difficulty holding ground, and seasonal limits on campaigning.
- The Roman-Parthian frontier settled into a long equilibrium because each side's military excelled on different terrain.

For three centuries after Carrhae, no Roman army crossed the Euphrates in full confidence. Emperors would try - Trajan, Verus, Severus - and some would take Ctesiphon, briefly. None would break Parthia. The riders with the composite bows and the armored lances had built something more durable than a single victory: a way of fighting matched to a way of living, that made the Iranian plateau, for as long as the dynasty held, nearly impossible to conquer. The next chapter moves from the battlefield to the road, from how the Parthians fought to what they defended - the commerce, cities, and cultural traffic that made those cavalry charges worth the saddle sores.

The theory of Parthian warfare - the composite bow, the armored lancer, the empire that summoned its cavalry from the saddle outward - is one thing on the page. It is another thing on a dusty plain in June, with the arrows falling and the water running out. For all its elegance as a system, Parthian military power entered Roman memory through a single catastrophe, one that froze the Euphrates frontier for three centuries. To see how the theory met practice, we have to walk onto the field at Carrhae itself.

Chapter 5:

Carrhae - The Day Rome Learned to Fear the East

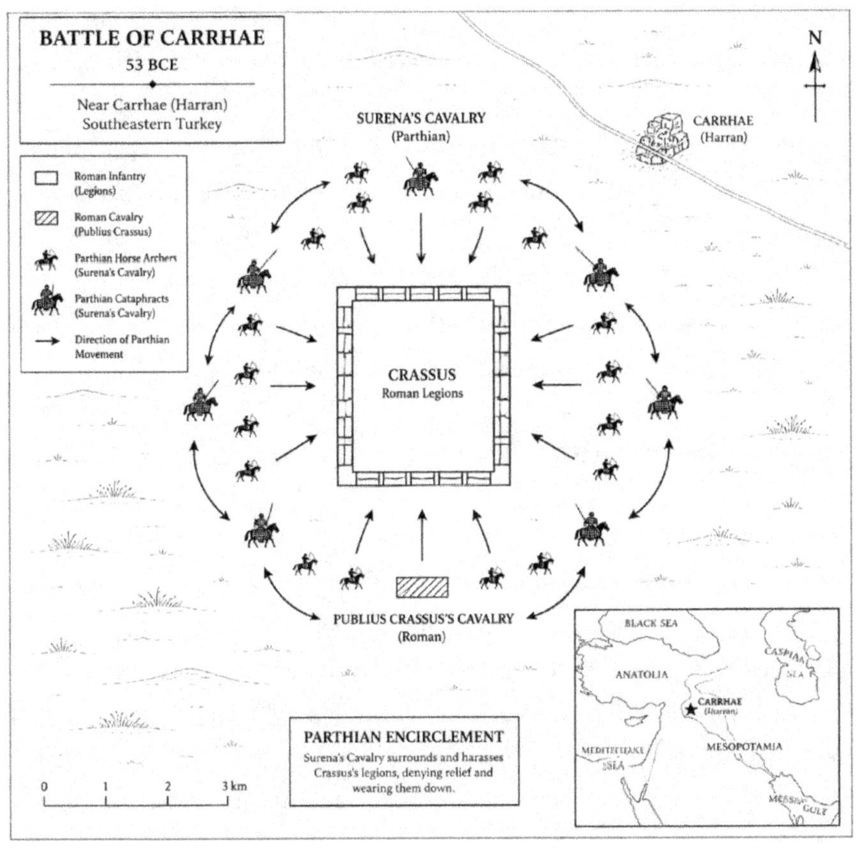

The Battle of Carrhae, 53 BCE

Marcus Licinius Crassus wanted a triumph to match Caesar's and Pompey's. Instead, in the summer heat of 53 BCE, he gave the Parthians one of the most lopsided victories in ancient history - and lost his head for his trouble.

For nearly two centuries, Rome had been accustomed to winning. Its legions had broken Carthage, humbled Macedon, trampled the Seleucid heirs of Alexander. When a sixty-year-old Roman grandee crossed the Euphrates at the head of seven legions, he assumed he was merely collecting the next province. What happened on the dusty plains near Carrhae was something the Roman imagination had scarcely prepared for: a total, annihilating defeat at the hands of a people most senators could not have reliably placed on a map. The shock reached into the marrow of the Republic. Eagles were lost. A consul's severed head became a stage prop in a Greek tragedy performed at a Parthian court. And a frontier that Rome had imagined as a line on the way to India hardened, almost overnight, into the edge of the known world. Carrhae is the hinge on which Roman attitudes toward the East pivoted from casual contempt to wary respect, and then to something closer to dread.

Crassus and the Politics of the First Triumvirate

To understand why a wealthy old man chose to gamble his life in the Syrian desert, one has to begin in Rome, where ambition was a kind of gravity. By the mid-50s BCE, Marcus Licinius Crassus was the richest man in the Republic, possibly the richest Rome had ever produced. He owned silver mines, slave schools, and whole neighborhoods whose burning he had personally profited from, having organized the city's first private fire brigade - a crew that often negotiated the sale price of a building while the flames climbed the walls.

Money, however, was not the same as glory. And in Rome, glory meant a triumph: the slow procession up the Capitoline, the captured kings, the cheering plebs. Crassus had scored one real military achievement, the suppression of Spartacus's slave revolt in 71 BCE, but Pompey had stolen much of the credit by mopping up the last rebel bands. Pompey had gone on to conquer the East as far as Judea. Julius Caesar, younger and hungrier, was then butchering his way through Gaul and dispatching letters home that read like serialized adventure fiction. Crassus, standing between these two giants, felt the pinch of comparison.

In 60 BCE he had helped engineer an informal political pact, later called the First Triumvirate, that bound the three men together in mutual advantage. They divided the Republic's spoils like a family cutting up an inheritance. At the conference of Luca in 56 BCE, the arrangement was renewed and refined. Caesar would keep Gaul. Pompey would manage Spain through deputies while remaining near Rome. Crassus, now in his sixties, would take Syria - and, by tacit understanding, use it as a launching pad against Parthia.

No senatorial decree authorized a Parthian war. Rome had treaties, however loose, with the Arsacid kings going back to Sulla's day. A tribune named Ateius Capito publicly cursed Crassus as he marched out of the city, pronouncing dire formulas over a brazier of burning herbs at the gates. Crowds muttered. Omens were reported. Crassus, who had never been superstitious in his business dealings, ignored them.

His motives were not purely vain. Parthia, in the Roman mental map, was a softer, richer version of the Seleucid kingdom that Pompey had dismembered. Its cities held legendary wealth. Its cavalry, Roman officers assumed, could not stand against disciplined heavy infantry any more than the armies of Tigranes or Mithridates had. Crassus reportedly spoke of pushing beyond the Euphrates to Bactria and perhaps to India, repeating the itinerary of Alexander. He was a sober man in most things, but he had allowed himself one romance. It would cost him everything.

The March into Mesopotamia

Crassus arrived in Syria in 54 BCE with seven legions, about four thousand cavalry, and a similar number of light infantry - perhaps forty thousand men in all. He spent the winter doing what Romans did best in a new province: counting. He weighed the treasures of the temple of Derceto at Hierapolis. He seized the gold reserves of the Jerusalem Temple, extracting from the high priest what Pompey had piously left untouched. To his soldiers this looked less like preparation for a war of conquest than like a grain merchant taking inventory.

The first probing campaign, in late 54 BCE, went well enough. Roman columns crossed the Euphrates at Zeugma, received the submission of several Greek-speaking cities of northern Mesopotamia, and installed garrisons. Had Crassus pressed on that autumn, before the Parthian king Orodes II could organize a response, the story might read differently. He did not. He pulled back across the river to winter in Syria, giving his opponent the most precious commodity in war: time.

Orodes used it carefully. He split his forces. He himself led the main army northwest into Armenia to punish King Artavasdes, who had been trying to persuade Crassus to take a mountain route through Armenian territory, where Parthian cavalry would be blunted by terrain. Against Crassus directly, Orodes dispatched his most gifted subordinate, a young aristocrat of the Suren clan whom Greek and Roman sources call simply Surena.

In the spring of 53 BCE, Crassus recrossed the Euphrates. Here the decisive choices were made, and here he made them badly. Artavasdes rode into the Roman camp in person and repeated his offer: come through Armenia, where cavalry cannot easily charge and where a friendly king can supply grain. Crassus refused. An Arab chieftain named Ariamnes - whom Roman writers, trying to assign blame, later painted as a deliberate Parthian agent - urged a direct march across the open plains southeast of the Euphrates, promising that the Parthians were already fleeing. Crassus listened to Ariamnes.

The legions left the river. They marched into a country of low, rolling ground, sparse grass, and no shade. Water grew scarce. The men ate cold rations as they walked. Officers began to grumble; Cassius Longinus, the quaestor - the same Cassius who would one day put a knife into Caesar - urged Crassus to keep the Euphrates on his flank for water and supply. Crassus overruled him. He had been told the enemy was running.

The enemy was not running. Surena, somewhere to the south, was shadowing the Roman column with a force that modern estimates place at around ten thousand: nine thousand horse archers and a thousand heavily armored lancers, the fearsome *cataphracts* whom the Greeks called clibanarii, men and horses alike encased in overlapping scale. Trailing the army was a baggage train of perhaps a thousand camels. Their cargo was not food. It was arrows.

On a morning in June, Roman scouts came galloping back to report that a large enemy force was closing from the south. The place where the columns met was near a small town called Carrhae, the biblical Haran, where Abraham had once paused on his way to Canaan. Few of the forty thousand Romans who deployed that day would ever see another sunset.

Surena and the Parthian Army

Surena was about thirty years old. Plutarch, our fullest source, describes him as the tallest and handsomest man in Parthia, which should perhaps be read less as a physical sketch than as a literary preparation for the fall of a Roman giant at the hands of an exotic prodigy. What is clear from Plutarch's account is that Surena came from one of the half-dozen great noble houses whose private armies and hereditary privileges held the Arsacid realm together. He had already distinguished himself by restoring Orodes to his throne after a civil war, storming the city of Seleucia on the Tigris in the process. He traveled, we are told, with two hundred wagons of concubines and a personal retinue of ten thousand slaves and retainers. He was the kind of subject a king ought to have worried about; Orodes would later worry a great deal.

The army Surena brought against Crassus was almost entirely mounted, and it encapsulated the military logic of the Parthian state. Arsacid Iran was a land of enormous distances, good pasture, and a warrior aristocracy that had ridden since childhood. It was poor, by comparison, in the sort of dense peasant populations from which Rome drew its legionaries. What it had instead was horses and the bow. Out of these it had built two complementary arms.

The first was the horse archer: a lightly armored rider on a fast, wiry steppe pony, carrying a powerful composite bow of wood, horn, and sinew. Such bows could drive an arrow through mail at close range and still bruise a man through padding at a hundred paces. Horse archers did not charge. They circled, shot, wheeled, and shot again. Most famously, they practiced the so-called Parthian shot: twisting in the saddle at full gallop to fire backward at a pursuing enemy, a maneuver so characteristic that the phrase has survived, garbled, into English as the "parting shot."

The second arm was the cataphract. These were the sons of the nobility, mounted on heavy horses bred on the Median plains, their riders sheathed from helm to ankle in iron or bronze scale, their mounts similarly armored. They carried a long two-handed lance, the *kontos*, capable of skewering two men at once. A cataphract charge was a battering ram. On its own, against disciplined infantry with room to maneuver, it could fail. In combination with archers who had already shredded formations and morale, it could end a battle.

Surena's genius at Carrhae was logistical as much as tactical. Horse archers consume arrows at a terrifying rate, and the conventional assumption among Roman and Greek commanders was that if one simply endured the first barrage under locked shields, the enemy would soon shoot his quivers dry and either retreat or close to melee, where armored infantry held the advantage. Surena knew this assumption and planned around it. He brought the camels. The supply train crouched just behind his lines, and riders detached in rotation to refill their quivers from its inexhaustible bundles. The arrows, that day, did not run out.

The Battle of Carrhae

Crassus formed his men in the Roman fashion for a battle on open ground: a great hollow square, twelve cohorts on each side, cavalry and light troops inside, baggage at the center. It was a prudent formation against an enemy who might try to turn a flank. Against a force that fought entirely at distance, it was a box delivering itself for target practice.

Surena opened the engagement with a trick. He kept his cataphracts hidden behind a screen of horse archers and ordered the archers to throw a cloak of dust and noise - drums covered in stretched hide and hung with bronze bells, whose deep rattling the Romans had never heard before. Plutarch describes legionaries going pale at the sound. Then the cataphracts revealed themselves in their armor of polished steel, and the archers fanned out to begin the work of the day.

The first Roman instinct was to charge. Skirmishers ran forward; the archers retreated beyond their reach and shot them down. Crassus ordered the legionaries to lock shields. The *testudo*, the famous tortoise, offered genuine protection from arrow fire. But the Parthian bows were heavy enough to pin shields to the forearms that held them and the feet that stood behind them. Men who lowered a shield to free a pinned hand were shot in the face. Those who did not were shot in the thigh.

Hours passed. The Romans waited, as soldiers had waited in a dozen previous eastern battles, for the arrows to slacken. They did not slacken. Word spread through the ranks that the enemy's supply was inexhaustible, and with it spread something that Roman armies were not used to feeling: the suspicion that discipline and endurance might not be enough.

Crassus ordered his son Publius, a capable young officer who had ridden with Caesar in Gaul, to take the Gallic cavalry - a thousand Celts given him for exactly such a purpose - along with a detachment of legionaries, and drive the archers back. Publius attacked with reckless courage. The Parthian archers fled, or seemed to. They drew him several miles from the main body, then turned, surrounded him, and shot his little command to pieces. The Gauls, lightly armored, tried to grapple with the cataphracts and were run through on the lances. Publius, wounded, ordered his shield-bearer to kill him. A Parthian rode back to the main battle carrying the younger Crassus's head on a spear.

They raised it where the father could see it. Plutarch's account of that moment is one of the most terrible in classical literature: the old man walking along the lines, trying to steady men who had just watched their general's son turned into a trophy, telling them the grief was his alone and their duty remained. It was a brave speech. It did not change the arithmetic.

The battle continued into dusk. The Parthians, unusually for ancient armies, did not press a night attack; Surena wanted his prize intact. In the darkness the Roman officers held a council and concluded that Crassus had lost his grip. They abandoned four thousand wounded, who were massacred the next morning, and retreated toward Carrhae. From there, harried by cavalry, they tried to reach the hills.

On the fourth day Surena offered a parley. Crassus, pushed forward by mutinous soldiers who threatened to surrender without him, rode out to meet the Parthian general. What happened next is disputed even in the ancient sources - whether a groom's horse bolted, whether an officer struck first, whether Surena had planned a killing all along. Swords came out. Crassus was cut down. His head and right hand were struck off and sent to Orodes in Armenia.

They arrived, according to Plutarch, during a performance of Euripides's *Bacchae* at the court of King Artavasdes, who had by then made peace with Parthia and was entertaining his new ally with Greek tragedy. The actor playing Agave - the mother who in her madness has killed her own son and carries his head onstage - seized Crassus's head from the messenger and delivered the climactic lines while brandishing it. The court roared. Whether the story is literally true or a Greek historian's perfect invention, it captures the moment precisely. Rome had sent a consul east; the East sent back a prop.

Aftermath: Eagles Lost and Lessons Learned

The numbers are stark. Of roughly forty thousand men who had followed Crassus across the Euphrates, about twenty thousand lay dead on the plain or along the road to the hills. Ten thousand were marched into captivity, many settled, according to later sources, as frontier garrisons on the eastern edge of the Parthian world near Merv. Perhaps ten thousand struggled back to Syria under Cassius, who organized the defense of the province with the cold competence that would one day make him the brain of a conspiracy against Caesar.

Worse, in Roman eyes, than the dead were the eagles. Each legion carried a silver standard shaped as the bird of Jupiter; to lose one was a disgrace that could end careers and haunt generations. At Carrhae, seven were lost. They went into Parthian temples. For more than thirty years, every Roman commander who looked east saw those captured standards in his mind. Augustus eventually recovered them, not by war but by diplomacy in 20 BCE, and he put that recovery on coins and on the breastplate of his own great statue at Prima Porta. A negotiated return of lost banners became one of the founding propaganda achievements of the Principate. That is how deep the wound went.

Politically, Carrhae tore a leg off the Triumvirate's stool. Crassus had been the balancer between Pompey and Caesar, a third weight that kept either from tipping into open war with the other. With him dead, the remaining two stared at each other across a narrowing distance. Within four years they were fighting at Pharsalus. The road from Carrhae to the Ides of March is not a straight one, but it is a real one.

For Parthia, the victory was double-edged. Surena had delivered the empire's greatest military triumph; Orodes promptly had him executed, unwilling to tolerate a subject of such prestige. The Arsacid state squandered much of the strategic advantage in subsequent years, failing to follow up decisively in Syria. But the psychological victory endured. Rome would invade Parthian territory again - under Antony, under Trajan, under Septimius Severus - and sometimes burn the capital at Ctesiphon. Rome would never, in three centuries of intermittent war, bring Parthia down.

The deeper lesson went beyond tactics. A Roman army, properly led and supplied, could be beaten on ground of an enemy's choosing by a foe who refused to fight the kind of battle Rome knew how to win. It was a lesson Rome's legions had taught others for two hundred years. At Carrhae they learned it themselves.

Key Figures & Events

Crassus was a financier who wanted to die a conqueror and managed only the second half of the plan. Surena was a young aristocrat who combined steppe cavalry traditions with a quartermaster's attention to arrows and camels. Orodes II was a king shrewd enough to divide his enemies and insecure enough to murder his own best general. The battle itself, fought over three or four days in June 53 BCE near the town that the Bible calls Haran, was less a contest than a demonstration. The parley that killed Crassus may have been a trap, a misunderstanding, or both; the result was the same.

Analysis

Why does Carrhae matter? Not because it changed a border; the frontier settled roughly on the Euphrates, where it had been drifting anyway. It matters because it changed a Roman assumption. Before Carrhae, the eastern world was, in the Roman imagination, a sequence of decaying Hellenistic kingdoms waiting to be harvested. After Carrhae, the East was a place where a different kind of war was possible - fought from horseback, won by logistics and patience, immune to the legion's usual remedies. That recognition shaped four hundred years of imperial strategy. It is why Augustus preferred treaties to campaigns, why Trajan's conquests evaporated, why Rome kept a permanent eastern army and not an eastern province of Mesopotamia.

Carrhae also reshaped Rome's sense of itself. A Republic that had grown used to explaining its dominance as the natural order of things had to absorb the fact that its dominance had limits, and that those limits had names: Surena, Orodes, the horse archer, the cataphract, the arrow-laden camel. Self-knowledge is often delivered by catastrophe.

Quick Summary

- Marcus Licinius Crassus, the wealthiest Roman of his age, invaded Parthia in 53 BCE seeking military glory to match Caesar and Pompey.
- He led roughly 40,000 troops across the Euphrates without Senate authorization, ignoring omens and the advice of the Armenian king.
- The Parthian general Surena met him with about 10,000 cavalry - horse archers backed by heavily armored cataphracts and a camel train of spare arrows.
- At Carrhae in June 53 BCE, Surena's archers shot the stationary Roman infantry apart; a counterattack led by Crassus's son Publius was annihilated.
- Crassus was killed during a parley; his head was reportedly used as a prop in a performance of Euripides at the Armenian court.
- Rome lost about 20,000 dead, 10,000 captured, and seven legionary eagles, which were not recovered until Augustus negotiated their return in 20 BCE.

- The defeat destabilized the First Triumvirate and helped clear the path to civil war between Caesar and Pompey.
- Surena, too successful for his king's comfort, was executed by Orodes II shortly afterward.

Carrhae was not the end of Roman ambitions in the East, but it was the end of Roman innocence about them. For the next three centuries, every emperor who rode toward the Euphrates carried the memory of those arrows, and every Parthian - and later Sasanian - commander knew that a determined horse-archer army could stop Rome cold. A single summer on a dusty plain had drawn a line across the map of the ancient world, a line the legions would push against, bleed along, and never finally cross.

Carrhae drew a line on the map, but it also exposed a pattern the Romans would come to count on. Surena, the general who had annihilated seven legions, was executed by his own king within months of his victory. The Arsacid house had a talent for destroying its most capable servants, and an even greater talent for destroying itself. Behind the disciplined cavalry and the clever diplomacy lay a dynasty that murdered its way through succession as a matter of routine. That machinery of violence deserves its own accounting.

Chapter 6:

Brothers, Rebels, and the Crisis of Succession

In 37 BCE, a Parthian prince named Phraates inherited his father's throne by the simplest method available to him: he killed his father, then killed his brothers, then killed his own son when the boy grew too popular. He would reign for thirty-five years. By Arsacid standards, this was not a scandal. It was a successful transition of power.

No institution defined the Parthian Empire more thoroughly than its ritual of succession, and none did more to weaken it. For four centuries, the Arsacid dynasty produced capable generals, shrewd diplomats, and cultured patrons - and then watched them tear each other apart in the palaces of Ctesiphon and Ecbatana. The Romans, who faced their own dynastic horrors, were still sometimes shocked by what they heard from the East. Yet Parthia's bloody successions were not a sign of barbarism or of a system broken. They were the system. Understanding how the Parthians chose their kings - and how often they unchose them - is essential to understanding why an empire that could repeatedly humiliate Rome on the battlefield could not stop humiliating itself at court. What follows traces the logic of Arsacid succession into its darkest corner: the reign of Phraates IV, a man who turned fratricide into policy.

No Rule of Primogeniture

The first thing to understand about the Parthian throne is that nobody agreed on who was supposed to sit on it. There was no law of primogeniture, no ironclad custom that the eldest son inherited. There was only a pool of eligible candidates - sons, brothers, nephews, cousins - and a contest, formal or informal, to decide among them.

This was not laziness on the part of the Arsacids. It reflected the political world they had inherited. Their dynasty had emerged from a confederation of horse-riding nomads on the Iranian plateau, where leadership had traditionally gone to the most capable adult male of a ruling lineage, not to the biological accident of firstborn sonship. When Arsaces I seized power in the mid-third century BCE, he brought that assumption with him. It suited a kingdom whose survival depended on the battlefield competence of its ruler. A nine-year-old heir was not much use when Seleucid armies were on the march.

So the Arsacids kept their options open. A dying king might designate a successor, but that designation was provisional. The nobility could ratify or reject it. Brothers of the dead king were legitimate contenders. So were brothers of the designated heir. So, sometimes, were ambitious cousins who could claim Arsacid blood and muster enough cavalry to make the claim stick.

The result was a system that optimized for one thing - the production of a ruler strong enough to hold the throne - at the cost of nearly everything else. Each succession became a stress test. Weak candidates were eliminated, often literally. Strong candidates emerged hardened by the fight. An Arsacid who took the throne after killing two brothers and exiling a third had already proven that he could outmaneuver rivals and command loyalty from the powerful families who had backed him.

This had obvious advantages and catastrophic disadvantages. It meant that the Parthian Empire was rarely ruled by children or fools. It also meant that every royal death was a detonation. Provinces rebelled. Nobles switched sides. Roman ambassadors watched the palaces of Seleucia with the eager attention of vultures, ready to back whichever contender might owe Rome a favor.

Compare this with the Roman imperial system that was taking shape during the same centuries. The Romans, for all their own dynastic chaos, at least tried to pretend they had rules. Adoptions were formalized, successors were groomed publicly, the Senate performed the rituals of ratification. The Parthians performed no such theater. They did not pretend the transfer of power was orderly. It wasn't, and everyone knew it.

What the Arsacids offered instead was a principle: the throne belonged to whichever Arsacid could take it and keep it. That principle produced Mithridates I, who expanded the empire to the Euphrates. It also produced Phraates IV, who murdered his father.

The Role of the Noble Council

The king did not rule alone, and he did not succeed alone. Behind every Arsacid on the throne stood the great noble houses of Parthia - the Suren, the Karin, the Mihran, and a handful of others - whose ancestors had been great before the Arsacids arrived and who fully expected to be great after they were gone.

These families controlled the east. They raised the cataphracts and horse archers that made Parthian armies feared. They held hereditary offices: the Suren, by ancient right, crowned each new king. Their estates spanned whole provinces. Their private armies could tip a civil war. And when a king died, they gathered in council to recognize - or refuse to recognize - his successor.

Greek and Roman sources speak of two councils advising the Parthian king, one of royal kinsmen and one of nobles and wise men, though the exact workings remain obscure. What is clear is that no Arsacid ruled without the consent of the great houses. A candidate who lacked their backing could not collect taxes, raise armies, or hold the frontier. A candidate they favored might seize the throne almost bloodlessly, even against the wishes of a dying king.

This was not constitutional government in any modern sense. It was closer to the elective monarchies of medieval Europe, or to the shifting loyalties of the Mongol khuriltai - a system in which aristocratic consensus mattered more than written law. The nobles chose, and their choice became legitimate through the ritual of coronation. If they chose badly, they could choose again.

For the Arsacids, this was both a ladder and a leash. A capable king could play the families against one another, rewarding loyalty with governorships and marriages, punishing sedition with exile or execution. A weak king became their puppet. Several Parthian monarchs who are little more than names in our sources seem to have been precisely that - figureheads placed on the throne because they were controllable, replaced when they became inconvenient.

The greatest of the houses, the Suren, produced the general who annihilated Crassus at Carrhae in 53 BCE. That victory made Surena, the family's standard-bearer, the most famous man in the empire. It also made him dangerous. King Orodes II, watching his vassal become a hero, had Surena executed soon afterward. The lesson was not lost on anyone. A noble who eclipsed his king might win battles; he would not live to enjoy the victory. A king who tolerated such an eclipse might not live either.

This mutual wariness between crown and nobility is the hidden engine of Parthian politics. Rome's frontier campaigns, Armenian intrigues, Jewish rebellions - all the headline events of Arsacid history took place against this background hum of aristocratic calculation. Every major decision at court involved, implicitly, the question: what will the great houses accept?

When they accepted a king, he ruled. When they did not, he died. And when they disagreed among themselves about who should rule, the empire came apart at the seams.

Phraates IV and the Murder of a Family

Orodes II, the conqueror of Crassus, outlived his triumph by a decade and a half. He was an old man by 37 BCE, broken by grief at the death of his favorite son Pacorus, who had been killed leading a Parthian army against the Romans in Syria the year before. Pacorus had been the designated heir, the bright future of the dynasty. His death left Orodes with a problem and his surviving sons with an opportunity.

There were many surviving sons - some sources say thirty, a figure surely exaggerated but suggestive of a royal harem that had been productive to the point of hazard. Among them was Phraates, ambitious, ruthless, and unwilling to wait. When Orodes, mourning and ill, hesitated to name a new heir, Phraates solved the problem for him. He murdered his father. Then he murdered his brothers - all of them, according to the sources - to eliminate every rival claim.

The new king took the throne as Phraates IV. His reign would last thirty-five years, longer than any Parthian ruler before him, and it opened with a demonstration that the butchery of his accession had been neither impulsive nor exceptional. When his eldest son grew into a young man popular with the nobility, Phraates had him killed too. The message was consistent: no rival would be allowed to exist, regardless of blood.

And then, against all reasonable expectations, Phraates IV proved to be a formidable king.

In 36 BCE, Mark Antony, Caesar's heir in the East, launched an enormous invasion of Parthia meant to avenge Carrhae and rival Alexander. Sixteen legions crossed into the Parthian sphere through Armenia. Phraates, barely a year on his blood-soaked throne, outmaneuvered them. His horse archers harried the Roman supply train. His cavalry destroyed the siege engines on which the entire campaign depended. Antony retreated through the Armenian mountains in winter and lost perhaps a third of his army to cold, hunger, and Parthian arrows. It was the worst Roman defeat since Carrhae, and it was administered by a parricide who had worn the crown for just over a year.

But Phraates' method of ruling - fear without affection - caught up with him. In 32 BCE, the nobility tired of his brutality and raised up a challenger, Tiridates, who briefly drove Phraates from his capital. Phraates fled east, recruited Scythian allies, and returned to reclaim his throne. Tiridates escaped to Roman territory, taking with him one of Phraates' young sons.

The rest of the reign was a long, wary dance with Augustus. In 20 BCE, Phraates returned the captured legionary standards taken at Carrhae - a concession Augustus celebrated on coins and monuments as a Roman victory, though no battle had been fought. A decade later, in 10 BCE, Phraates did something stranger: he sent four of his surviving sons to live in Rome as honored hostages. The official reason, pressed on him by his Italian concubine Musa, was diplomatic goodwill. The real reason was paranoia. Four sons in Rome were four sons who could not plot in Ctesiphon.

Musa herself had begun her career as a gift from Augustus to the Parthian court. She rose from concubine to queen, bore Phraates a son named Phraataces, and spent years persuading her husband to clear the path for him. In 2 BCE, she completed the work. Phraates IV, the man who had murdered his father and brothers and eldest son to secure the throne, was poisoned by his wife and surviving boy. Phraataces took the crown. He would not keep it long.

Civil Wars as a Feature, Not a Bug

Historians looking back on the Arsacid dynasty sometimes treat its civil wars as symptoms of decline - the visible cracks in a failing state. This gets the story backwards. Parthian civil wars were not malfunctions. They were how the system worked.

Consider the arithmetic. In four hundred and seventy years of Arsacid rule, fewer than a third of the kings died peacefully of natural causes while still on the throne. The rest were murdered, deposed, killed in battle, or forced into exile. At several points, two or three men simultaneously claimed the title King of Kings, each minting coins, each commanding armies, each controlling portions of the empire.

And yet the empire endured. Through each cycle of fratricide and rebellion, the Arsacid name retained its legitimacy. The great houses continued to recognize Arsacids as the only acceptable rulers. When the dynasty finally fell in 224 CE, it was not because the civil wars had hollowed it out from within but because a new power from Persia, the Sasanians, was strong enough to replace it.

Why did the system persist? Because it delivered what the Parthian world demanded: rulers who had proven themselves. A king who emerged from a three-way civil war had shown he could command loyalty, organize armies, negotiate with nobles, and make hard decisions under pressure. These were the skills required to hold a frontier against Rome and govern a polyglot empire stretching from Mesopotamia to the Hindu Kush. A peacefully inherited throne produced no such guarantees.

The costs were real. Civil wars devastated provinces. Rebellious nobles burned rival cities. Roman armies exploited every succession crisis, backing one Arsacid contender against another. Armenia, the eternal buffer state, changed hands with every convulsion. Economic damage accumulated. Border zones slipped out of central control.

But these costs were borne unevenly. The core of the empire - the noble estates, the trade routes, the caravan cities - mostly survived. Civil war at the top rarely meant civil war in the countryside. A peasant in Media might know that Ctesiphon had changed hands; he rarely had to care. Tribute flowed to whoever held the capital. Tax collectors kept collecting. The system absorbed its convulsions.

What the Arsacids built, almost by accident, was an empire whose political instability at the top coexisted with remarkable stability at the middle and bottom. The noble houses endured for centuries. The cities kept their privileges. The trade routes pumped silk and silver regardless of which prince was winning. It was, in its strange way, a functioning arrangement - ugly, violent, efficient.

It was also why Rome, despite enormous material advantages, could never conquer Parthia. Every Roman invasion hoped to exploit a succession crisis. Sometimes they succeeded tactically, installing a client king or capturing a province. But the Arsacid system was shock-resistant in a way the Romans never quite understood. Kill a Parthian king and another emerged, bloodied but legitimate. Back a pretender and he would be absorbed or destroyed by the next round of the internal contest. The empire refused to stay wounded.

Key Figures & Events

- **Orodes II**: Victor of Carrhae, reportedly murdered by his son Phraates IV around 37 BCE after the death of his favored heir Pacorus.
- **Phraates IV (r. 37-2 BCE)**: Perhaps the most feared of Arsacid kings, killer of his father, brothers, and eldest son; defeated Mark Antony in 36 BCE.
- **Mark Antony's Invasion (36 BCE)**: Catastrophic Roman campaign that confirmed Phraates IV's grip on power and humiliated Rome's most famous general.
- **Tiridates' Revolt (32-30 BCE)**: Noble-backed rebellion that briefly drove Phraates from his throne, demonstrating the fragility of even a strong king's position.
- **The Hostage Princes (10 BCE)**: Four of Phraates' sons sent to Rome, a diplomatic gesture disguising a deeply paranoid calculation.

- **Musa and Phraataces (2 BCE)**: Assassination of Phraates IV by his Italian-born queen and their son, ending one of the longest Arsacid reigns.

Analysis

The violent peculiarities of Arsacid succession look less like chaos and more like a functional, if brutal, selection mechanism when set against the Parthian strategic environment. An empire squeezed between Rome and the steppe, dependent on cavalry aristocracy and regional warlords, could not afford incompetent kings. The Arsacid system ensured it rarely got them.

But the same mechanism that filtered out weaklings made every succession a wound, and those wounds accumulated. Roman generals learned to wait for Parthian civil wars and march in during the turmoil. Armenian kings switched allegiance based on which Arsacid looked likelier to win. Noble houses grew increasingly assertive, knowing that each new king owed them something. By the second century CE, the pattern of fragmentation was becoming harder to reverse.

Phraates IV is the dynasty in miniature. He achieved the throne by unspeakable crime and then used it to defeat Rome's greatest general. He survived revolt, cultivated a delicate peace with Augustus, and built the longest reign in Arsacid history. And he died by the hand of his own wife and son, following the logic he himself had authored. The system produced kings strong enough to save the empire, and it killed them before they could save themselves.

Quick Summary

- The Arsacid dynasty had no fixed rule of primogeniture; succession was contested among all eligible male Arsacids.

- Great noble houses - Suren, Karin, Mihran, and others - held the real power to ratify or reject kings.
- Phraates IV seized the throne in 37 BCE by murdering his father Orodes II, his brothers, and later his eldest son.
- Despite his brutality, Phraates defeated Mark Antony's massive invasion in 36 BCE, one of Rome's worst defeats.
- In 10 BCE, Phraates sent four sons to Rome as hostages to prevent them from challenging him at home.
- He was assassinated in 2 BCE by his Italian-born queen Musa and their son Phraataces.
- Civil wars were not dysfunction but the core Arsacid mechanism for selecting capable rulers.
- The system produced strong kings but left the empire perpetually vulnerable during succession crises.

The Parthian throne devoured its occupants for nearly five centuries, and yet the empire they ruled outlasted the Roman Republic and every Hellenistic kingdom combined. The Arsacids had made a bargain with violence, and for a long time the bargain held. But every bargain comes due. The succession crises that had once produced kings like Phraates IV would eventually produce only exhaustion - and in the third century, when a Persian nobleman named Ardashir rose against a weakened Arsacid king, he would find a dynasty still capable of murder but no longer capable of renewal. That story lay centuries in the future. For now, the riders still held the East, and the Romans still watched the palaces of Ctesiphon with their vultures' patience, waiting for the next brother to lift a knife.

The knife in the succession chamber is only half the story. For all the brothers who killed brothers at Ctesiphon, the city itself kept functioning, its markets filling, its scribes writing, its arch rising above the Tigris. The Arsacid bargain with violence was survivable precisely because the empire was more than its court. It rested on a dense urban network that the kings had inherited from older civilizations and adapted to their own purposes. To see what the murderous princes actually ruled, we need to step outside the palace and into the streets.

Chapter 7:

Ctesiphon and the Cities of the Empire

Stand on the east bank of the Tigris, in the flat alluvial plain south of modern Baghdad, and you are standing on what was once one of the largest cities on Earth. The mud has swallowed most of it. A single enormous arch still rises from the dust, the tallest unreinforced brick vault ever built by human hands.

That arch belonged to Ctesiphon, the winter capital of the Parthian kings and, later, their Sasanian successors. But Ctesiphon was only one node in a sprawling urban network that the Arsacid dynasty inherited, adapted, and expanded across five centuries. From the oasis fortresses of Turkmenistan to the old Achaemenid metropolises of the Iranian plateau and the Greek foundations of Mesopotamia, the Parthians ruled through cities they did not always build but almost always tolerated. Their empire was not a single capital with a single language. It was an archipelago of royal residences, Hellenistic poleis, caravan towns, and temple complexes, loosely stitched together by roads, rivers, and the court's migratory rhythm. To understand how the Parthians held their superpower together, you have to understand the cities where Greek met Aramaic, where an Iranian king might watch a performance of Euripides, and where a new kind of architecture was being invented one brick at a time.

The Twin Cities of the Tigris

Seleucia-on-the-Tigris was already a giant when the Parthians arrived. Founded around 305 BCE by Seleucus I, one of Alexander's generals, it had been designed as the eastern counterweight to Antioch. Greek colonists filled its grid of streets. Its population, by some ancient estimates, reached six hundred thousand, making it one of the three or four largest cities in the world. It had a Greek-style council, theaters, gymnasia, and the full machinery of a polis transplanted to Mesopotamian soil.

When Mithridates I took the city in 141 BCE, and when his nephew Mithridates II consolidated Parthian control in the late second century, the dynasty faced a choice. They could garrison Seleucia and rule from inside its walls, alienating its Greek citizens. Or they could leave Seleucia largely to govern itself and build something new nearby. They chose the second option, and it was a masterstroke of imperial politics.

Directly across the river from Seleucia, on the east bank of the Tigris, the Parthians raised Ctesiphon. It began, probably, as a military camp - a place for the royal army to winter without provoking Seleucia's merchant class. It grew into a royal residence, then a court city, then a capital. By the first century CE, Ctesiphon had eclipsed its older neighbor in political importance while Seleucia remained the commercial and Greek-cultural heart of the region. Contemporaries spoke of them almost as a single entity. Pliny the Elder noted that the Parthians built Ctesiphon specifically to draw traffic away from Seleucia, and then, when that failed, founded yet a third town, Vologasias, nearby.

The result was a kind of urban hydra on the Tigris. Greek-speakers ran their own civic affairs on the west bank. Iranian aristocrats and the royal entourage occupied the east. Aramaic-speaking merchants and farmers filled the countryside in between. Jewish communities, already rooted in Mesopotamia since the Babylonian exile, flourished in both cities and in nearby towns like Nehardea and later Pumbedita, where the great Babylonian Talmudic academies would eventually arise. Zoroastrian fire priests, Babylonian astronomers, and itinerant philosophers all found patrons within a few miles of one another.

Ctesiphon's geography did much of the political work. The Tigris carried grain and goods; the roads from Ecbatana to Syria passed through the plain;

the royal armies could muster here before marching west against Rome or east to police the Iranian nobility. When Trajan's legions broke through in 114 CE and briefly occupied the city, they found palaces, treasuries, and a royal golden throne that the emperor reportedly carried off as a trophy. Rome would return three more times over the next century - under Lucius Verus, Septimius Severus, and eventually Caracalla - and each sack revealed how much wealth had accumulated on the Tigris's eastern bank.

Yet the city kept rebuilding. The same flatness that made Ctesiphon vulnerable also made it cheap to reconstruct, and the Parthian administration, nomadic in its origins, had never relied on a single fixed capital. Ctesiphon was grand but replaceable. That was its paradox: the largest city in the empire was also, in a sense, one among many.

Nisa: The Ancestral Heartland

Long before Ctesiphon, there was Nisa. Tucked against the Kopet Dag mountains in what is now southern Turkmenistan, near the modern city of Ashgabat, Nisa was the cradle of Arsacid power. Here, in the mid-third century BCE, Arsaces I and his followers established themselves as rulers of the satrapy of Parthia after breaking away from Seleucid authority. The site consists of two mounds - Old Nisa and New Nisa - and archaeologists have spent more than a century teasing out what they meant to the dynasty.

Old Nisa was not an ordinary town. It appears to have been a royal and dynastic complex, a kind of sacred precinct where the Arsacids honored their ancestors, stored their treasures, and staged ceremonies of legitimacy. Mithridates I, who reigned from 171 to 138 BCE and transformed Parthia from a regional kingdom into a Near Eastern empire, renamed the site Mithradatkirt, "Mithridates's Fortress." The name broadcast an idea: this was the king's own place, inseparable from the house of Arsaces.

What Soviet and later Turkmen archaeologists uncovered at Old Nisa astonished them. Columned halls built in a recognizably Hellenistic idiom, with capitals echoing Greek orders, stood alongside rooms decorated with unmistakably Iranian motifs. Clay statues, some nearly life-sized, depicted robed figures whose identities remain debated - perhaps ancestral kings, perhaps deities, perhaps both. More than fifty rhytons, ceremonial drinking horns carved from ivory, bore scenes from Greek mythology: centaurs, satyrs, Dionysiac revels. And thousands of ostraca, potsherds inscribed in Aramaic script but in an Iranian language, recorded the wine deliveries that flowed into the royal cellars from estates across the region.

Those ostraca are among the most revealing documents of early Parthian rule. They show a bureaucracy that used Aramaic letters to write Parthian words - a habit inherited from the Achaemenid administrative tradition and carried forward for centuries. They show a court that consumed wine in quantities suggesting serious feasting. And they show an economy organized around royal estates and their tribute, funneling produce from the Kopet Dag foothills into the king's storehouses.

Nisa mattered symbolically long after the court's political center shifted westward to Ctesiphon. The Arsacids never forgot that they were horsemen from the northeast, and the dynasty's legitimacy was rooted in this landscape of oases and mountain passes. Even when the king spent most of his year in Mesopotamia, Nisa remained a ceremonial anchor - the place the dynasty came from, the place its ancestors were remembered. The Parthian Empire had, in this sense, two hearts. The political one beat on the Tigris. The older one beat against the Kopet Dag.

Hecatompylos, Ecbatana, Susa

Between the two hearts lay a string of cities that no Parthian ruler could afford to ignore. The Parthians did not so much inhabit a single capital as rotate through a circuit of them, following the seasons and the demands of politics. The king's court moved. The administration moved with it.

Hecatompylos, whose Greek name means "the city of a hundred gates," sat in north-central Iran, probably near modern Damghan. It had been a Seleucid foundation, and the Parthians adopted it as one of their earliest major capitals, convenient for a dynasty still oriented toward the northeast. From here the Arsacids could command the great east-west road that would later be called the Silk Road, watching caravans move between Bactria and Mesopotamia. Ancient sources describe Hecatompylos as large and prosperous, though its ruins have been only partially excavated and much remains guesswork.

Ecbatana, by contrast, was a city with deep memory. Nestled in the Zagros at the site of modern Hamadan, it had been the summer capital of the Medes, then of the Achaemenids, then of the Seleucids. Its elevation - around 1,800 meters - made it cool in summer when the Mesopotamian plain was an oven, and the Parthian kings, following a tradition older than their dynasty, used it as their warm-weather residence. Court, treasury, and harem migrated there each year. The Greek historian Polybius described Ecbatana's palace as extraordinarily rich, its columns plated in silver and gold - plating that successive conquerors, including Alexander, had already begun to strip. By the Parthian era, the palace was less dazzling, but the city's administrative importance endured.

Susa, down in the lowlands of Khuzestan, was older still. A great city when Babylon was young, it had served as a capital of Elam and then of the Achaemenid kings who built their most famous palace there. The Parthians inherited Susa and treated it with the respect due to an ancient place. They allowed it to function as a Greek-style polis, minting its own coins, keeping its own civic institutions, and sending the occasional Greek inscription to the royal court. One such inscription, from the reign of Artabanus III in the first century CE, records a local petition and the king's reply - evidence that Parthian rulers corresponded with their cities in Greek and took civic concerns seriously.

Other cities filled out the network. Rhagae near modern Tehran. Charax Spasinou at the head of the Persian Gulf, a crucial node for maritime trade with India. Assur on the Tigris, revived under Parthian patronage after centuries of decline. Dura-Europos on the Euphrates, a Macedonian colony that became a Parthian frontier town and later fell to Rome. Each had its own languages, its own gods, its own local aristocracy. The Arsacids did not try to homogenize them. They collected tribute, demanded military service from the nobility, and otherwise let the cities run themselves.

Urban Life and Multilingual Communities

Walk into a Parthian city in, say, 50 CE, and the first thing you would notice is the languages. Greek on inscriptions and coins, still the prestige language of administration and trade. Aramaic in everyday writing, the lingua franca inherited from the Persian and Babylonian past. Parthian - an Iranian language written in Aramaic script - in royal and aristocratic circles. Akkadian still hanging on in Babylonian temples, where priests copied cuneiform tablets of astronomical observations into the first century CE. Hebrew in synagogues. Syriac emerging as a Christian liturgical language by the second century. In the bazaars, you would hear Bactrian traders, Arab caravaneers, and Indian merchants negotiating in whatever pidgin worked.

This multilingualism was not accidental. The Parthians had inherited from the Seleucids a model of urban autonomy that suited their own preferences. Greek cities kept their councils and assemblies. Babylonian temples kept their estates and their priesthoods. Jewish communities kept their courts. The king sent a representative, collected revenues, and intervened mainly when factions inside a city appealed to him or when external threats demanded a military response.

Jewish life in particular flourished under this arrangement. Mesopotamia had been home to a large Jewish population since the sixth-century BCE exile, and under Parthian rule that population grew, prospered, and developed the institutions that would produce, centuries later, the Babylonian Talmud. Rabbinic tradition remembered the Arsacids warmly, in pointed contrast to Rome. When Rome sacked the Temple in Jerusalem in 70 CE, Parthia offered a refuge. Jewish exilarchs - civic leaders of the community - operated with quasi-royal dignity inside the empire.

Greek communities, too, retained a remarkable vitality. Parthian kings styled themselves *philhellene* - friend of the Greeks - on their coins for generations. A famous anecdote from Plutarch describes the Parthian court watching a performance of Euripides's *Bacchae* at the wedding of a royal son around 53 BCE, with the severed head of the Roman general Crassus brought onstage as a prop. The story is lurid, but the cultural detail is telling. Parthian nobles knew their Euripides. They staged Greek tragedy in Greek. They built theaters.

Religious life was equally plural. Zoroastrian fire temples operated across the Iranian plateau, and some scholars argue that Vologases I in the mid-first century CE took an active role in compiling Zoroastrian oral traditions. Parthian coins also show Greek gods - Tyche, Apollo, Heracles - and local cults thrived in every province. Temples to Bel and Nabu continued at Babylon. Palmyrene merchants worshipped their own triad of gods. At Hatra, an Arab client kingdom inside the Parthian sphere, a vast temple complex honored the sun god Shamash and a pantheon that mixed Mesopotamian, Arab, and Iranian elements.

This was not tolerance in the modern liberal sense. It was pragmatic imperial management by a dynasty that understood it could not rule a space this diverse by force alone. Let the cities keep their gods and their laws. Collect the taxes. Call up the cavalry when needed. The system worked for nearly five hundred years.

Architecture: The Iwan and Its Legacy

Walk through the ruins of a Parthian royal building, and one form keeps appearing: a great vaulted hall, open at one end, rectangular in plan, often set against an interior courtyard. The Persians would later call it an *iwan*. It may be the Parthians' most lasting gift to world architecture.

The iwan was not entirely their invention. Precedents existed in earlier Mesopotamian and Iranian buildings. But the Parthians developed it into a signature element, deploying it in palaces, temples, and ceremonial complexes from Assur to Nisa to Ctesiphon. The form had practical virtues. A deep vaulted hall open on one side caught the cool evening breeze while offering shade during the day. It also provided a stage for the king: visitors approaching across an open courtyard saw the monarch framed inside the arch, elevated, haloed by shadow. Ceremony and climate met in a single architectural idea.

The greatest surviving Parthian-style iwan is actually Sasanian, built at Ctesiphon in the sixth century CE on the foundations of earlier Parthian work. The Taq Kasra, as it is known, still stands - a brick arch thirty-seven meters high, its span the widest of any unreinforced brick vault in the world. Earthquakes, floods, and centuries of plunder have reduced the surrounding palace to rubble, but the arch holds. To stand beneath it is to feel what a Parthian or Sasanian subject must have felt when summoned before the king of kings.

Parthian builders achieved these spans through mastery of baked brick and mortar, techniques refined in Mesopotamia over thousands of years but pushed to new scales. They decorated their walls with carved stucco panels - geometric patterns, vine scrolls, hunting scenes, winged figures - that anticipated the lush surface ornament of later Islamic architecture.

The legacy traveled. When the Sasanians supplanted the Arsacids in 224 CE, they inherited the iwan and made it the centerpiece of their own royal style.

When Islamic dynasties rose on the ruins of Sasanian Iran, they adopted the form again, placing iwans at the four sides of mosque courtyards from Isfahan to Samarkand to Delhi. The Taj Mahal's great entrance archway is, in its deepest ancestry, a Parthian idea. So is the portal of nearly every classical Persian mosque. A nomadic dynasty from the steppes of Central Asia, ruling a multilingual empire of inherited cities, left behind an architectural grammar that would shape the Islamic world for the next thousand years. It is among the strangest and most beautiful ironies of their story.

Analysis

The Parthian urban system tells us something important about how premodern empires actually worked. Rome, with its Latin administration, its citizenship law, its uniform army, projected an image of cultural and legal unity that modern Europeans have found easy to romanticize. Parthia projected no such image, and for that reason historians long underestimated it. But Parthia's loose, layered, multilingual approach was not a weakness. It was a sophisticated answer to the problem of governing a space where Greek cities, Iranian aristocrats, Aramaic scribes, Jewish academies, and Arab temple-kingdoms all had to coexist.

The Arsacids did not force the pieces together. They let them fit. Ctesiphon rose not by crushing Seleucia but by sitting beside it. Nisa persisted as a dynastic shrine while the real work of government happened a thousand miles away. Ecbatana cooled the court in summer. Susa processed petitions in Greek. The iwan framed the king's authority in architectural terms that everyone, regardless of language, could read.

That flexibility was the empire's genius, and ultimately also its limit. When the Sasanians came to power, they built a more centralized, more ideologically unified state, with Zoroastrianism as a quasi-state religion and Middle Persian as the dominant administrative language. They remembered the Parthians with some disdain, as a dynasty that had let too many things drift. But the cities the Parthians had nurtured, and the architectural forms they had perfected, outlived them by centuries. The Parthian empire was, in a sense, less a kingdom than a network - and networks are harder to destroy than kingdoms.

Quick Summary

- The Parthians built Ctesiphon on the east bank of the Tigris opposite the Greek city of Seleucia, creating a twin-city complex that combined Iranian royal power with Greek commercial and civic life.
- Nisa, in modern Turkmenistan, served as the dynastic and ceremonial heartland of the Arsacids and was renamed Mithradatkirt by Mithridates I.
- The Parthian court rotated seasonally between Ctesiphon, Ecbatana, Hecatompylos, and Susa, each with its own languages, institutions, and traditions.
- Parthian cities hosted Greek, Aramaic, Parthian, Hebrew, Akkadian, Syriac, and other linguistic communities, which the dynasty allowed to govern themselves under loose royal oversight.
- Jewish communities flourished in Mesopotamia under Parthian rule, laying the groundwork for the later Babylonian Talmudic academies.
- The Parthians developed the iwan, a vaulted open-fronted hall that would become a defining element of Sasanian and later Islamic architecture.
- Rome repeatedly sacked Ctesiphon - under Trajan in 114 CE and later emperors - but the city was always rebuilt, reflecting the resilience of Parthia's decentralized urban network.

The cities of the Parthian Empire do not survive the way Rome's do. There is no Parthian Colosseum, no Parthian Pantheon still hosting worshippers. What survives instead is an idea about how to rule diversity without demanding uniformity, and a single enormous arch on the Tigris that still tells anyone who stands beneath it that something vast once happened here. When Muslim armies swept across this landscape six centuries later and began raising their own cities and mosques, they built on Parthian foundations - sometimes literally, often architecturally, always within a world the riders from the steppe had helped to shape.

Ctesiphon did not grow rich on river water alone. The cities of the Arsacid empire, from Seleucia to Merv, were thickened by something the Parthians controlled almost by accident of geography: the long overland roads that carried Chinese silk west and Roman glass east. The arch on the Tigris was paid for, in part, by every camel train that crossed the Iranian plateau. To understand the wealth that held the empire together, and the quiet power it gave Arsacid kings over markets they never saw, we have to follow the caravans.

Chapter 8:

Silk, Spice, and the Arsacid Middlemen

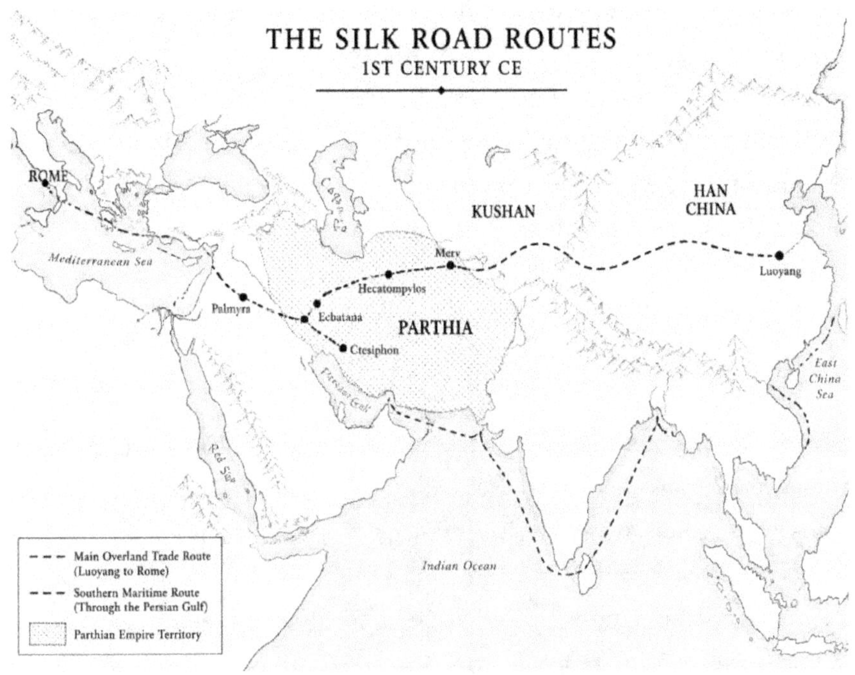

The Silk Road: Parthia at the Center, c. 1st Century CE

A bolt of Chinese silk, loaded onto a camel in Gansu, might change hands a dozen times before a Roman senator's wife draped it across her shoulders in Ostia. At every exchange, somebody took a cut. More often than not, that somebody answered to an Arsacid king.

Geography had handed the Parthians a gift that no amount of military valor could have won on its own. Their empire stretched across the narrow waist of Eurasia, the one zone through which almost all overland traffic between China and the Mediterranean had to squeeze. To the north lay the steppe, hostile and trackless. To the south lay desert and sea. In between ran the caravan roads, and the Parthians owned them. For nearly five centuries, the Arsacids perfected the quiet art of the middleman - taxing, guiding, protecting, occasionally plundering, and always profiting from a commerce whose volume astonished contemporaries and still astonishes us. What follows traces the goods as they moved: silk from the looms of Han China, frankincense from Arabia, pepper from India, glass from Syria, and silver from the mines of Iberia. It traces the men who walked beside the camels and the kings who counted the customs receipts. And it asks a hard question the Romans themselves asked with mounting anger: where was all the gold going?

The Silk Road in the Parthian Period

The phrase "Silk Road" was coined in the nineteenth century by a German geographer, and it has the drawback of suggesting a single highway. There was no highway. There was a web of trails, river crossings, mountain passes, and walled caravanserais that contracted and expanded according to weather, banditry, and politics. What held the web together during the Parthian centuries was a stretch of roughly two thousand miles of Arsacid-controlled territory running from Merv in the east to Seleucia on the Tigris in the west.

We know the shape of this network in unusual detail because a Parthian Greek named Isidore of Charax sat down in the first century BCE and wrote it out. His short work, *Parthian Stations*, is essentially an itinerary - a list of the staging posts along the main route from the Euphrates to the frontier of India, with distances given in *schoeni* and occasional notes on local features. It is one of the great survivals of ancient geography: a dry, practical document that happens to be a near-complete map of the trunk road of a superpower.

Isidore's route ran from Zeugma on the Euphrates, down through Seleucia-Ctesiphon, across the Zagros by way of the old royal road, and on through Ecbatana, Rhagae near modern Tehran, and the Caspian Gates to Hecatompylos. From there it branched northeast to Merv and the Oxus, and southeast toward Arachosia and the passes into India. Every stage was a day's march or two - enough to water camels and men, collect tolls, and push on.

The caravans themselves were substantial enterprises. A train of several hundred camels, each carrying perhaps five hundred pounds, represented a small fortune on the hoof. They moved at the pace of the slowest animal, roughly twenty miles a day on good ground. A journey from the Chinese frontier to Mesopotamia took the better part of a year, and no single merchant walked the whole distance. Instead, goods passed through relays of traders - Sogdians in the east, Bactrians and Parthians in the middle, Syrians and Jews and Palmyrenes toward the west - each specializing in a segment he knew intimately.

What moved along these trails was not only silk. Chinese lacquerware, bronze mirrors, and rhubarb root traveled west. Indian pepper, cotton, indigo, and gemstones joined the westbound flow where the routes from the subcontinent fed in. Heading east went Roman glass, which the Chinese prized and could not yet make to the same quality, along with red coral, woolen textiles, linen, amber from the Baltic, and the silver denarii that eventually reached Chinese hoards. Horses from Ferghana - the famous "blood-sweating" breed that obsessed the Han court - moved east into China as a strategic commodity. Slaves moved in both directions.

The Parthians did not need to produce any of this themselves. They needed only to keep the roads open, the wells dug, the bandits intimidated, and the customs houses staffed. Archaeology has turned up caravanserais with stabling for hundreds of animals, fortified posts where documents were checked, and the remains of weigh-stations where duties were assessed. One estimate, based on fragmentary evidence from the Roman side, puts the overland tariff at roughly a quarter of a cargo's value by the time it reached the Mediterranean. Multiply that across the annual volume, and one can see why the Arsacid treasury rarely ran short.

Critics have said the Parthians contributed nothing to civilization. What they contributed was a long, stable corridor through which civilizations could talk to each other. That was not nothing.

The First Chinese Embassy: Zhang Qian and After

The opening of the road had an author, and his name was Zhang Qian. In 138 BCE, the Han emperor Wu dispatched this young officer on an errand that was military before it was commercial: he was to find the Yuezhi, a nomadic people driven west by the Xiongnu, and persuade them to join the Han in a pincer attack on their common enemy. Zhang Qian was captured by the Xiongnu almost at once, held for a decade, escaped, pressed on across the Pamirs, reached the Yuezhi in Bactria, and found them comfortably settled and entirely uninterested in a war of revenge. He came home in 126 BCE, thirteen years after he had set out, with one of the two original companions he had started with and a head full of information.

That information changed everything. Zhang Qian described to the Han court a world the Chinese had not known existed: settled kingdoms of enormous wealth, with walled cities, irrigated agriculture, and markets where one could buy goods from lands still further west. He named Anxi - the Chinese transcription of "Arsaces" - as a powerful kingdom of traders whose coins bore the faces of their kings and who stood athwart the road to Rome.

A second mission, around 119 BCE, went further. Zhang Qian this time led a large embassy carrying gifts, and he sent subordinates on to Anxi itself. The Parthian king - probably Mithridates II, then at the height of his power - understood exactly what was being offered. He sent ambassadors back to

Chang'an with gifts of their own: ostrich eggs and, according to the Han annalists, conjurers from Alexandria. Silk began to move west in quantity. Chinese bronze and lacquer trickled into Parthian hands. The two empires never shared a border, but they had opened a conversation that would continue, through intermediaries, for four hundred years.

The Parthians seem to have grasped a point that would frustrate Rome for centuries: if you sat in the middle, you had an interest in keeping the ends apart. Later Chinese sources record an embassy in 97 CE, sent by the Han general Ban Chao under the command of an envoy named Gan Ying, who was supposed to reach Rome directly. Gan Ying got as far as the Persian Gulf. There, according to the *Book of the Later Han*, Parthian sailors talked him out of the voyage by describing a sea crossing so terrible - storms, homesickness, death - that he turned back. The account is almost certainly propaganda. The Parthians did not want the Han meeting the Romans face to face. A direct channel would have cut them out of their most lucrative trade.

Instead, the two ends of the road knew each other only through rumor. Roman authors wrote of the *Seres*, the silk people, as shadowy, just, long-lived, and remote. Chinese authors wrote of Da Qin, the great Qin, a western empire of fabulous wealth and honest officials. Neither was entirely wrong. Neither could get past Ctesiphon.

Ports of the Persian Gulf and Characene

Not everything moved by camel. A great deal moved by ship, and for maritime commerce the Parthians possessed an asset almost as valuable as the land corridor: the head of the Persian Gulf.

At the mouth of the Tigris and Euphrates lay the small kingdom of Characene, or Mesene, with its capital at Spasinou Charax. Officially a vassal of the Arsacids, Characene functioned as a semi-autonomous port authority, minting its own coinage, hosting Greek-speaking merchants, and handling the seaborne traffic that linked Mesopotamia to India and the Arabian coast. Isidore of Charax, the geographer of the caravan route, took his name from this city. It was a place where a literate man with a head for distances could make a living.

Ships sailing out of Charax caught the monsoon winds down the Gulf, past the pearl fisheries of Bahrain, and into the Arabian Sea. By the first century CE the monsoon system was well understood, and vessels could make the crossing to the Indian ports of Barbaricon, at the mouth of the Indus, and Barygaza on the Gujarat coast within a single sailing season. From India came pepper - the dominant spice of the Roman kitchen - along with cotton textiles, steel, ivory, tortoiseshell, sandalwood, and semi-precious stones. Outbound went dates, Mesopotamian grain, Parthian horses, wine, and, increasingly, Roman silver.

The Gulf route competed with, and sometimes complemented, the Red Sea route that Rome had developed through Egypt. Roman emperors liked the Red Sea option because it bypassed Parthian territory entirely. Merchants, however, often found the Gulf more attractive: Characene's warehouses were closer to the overland markets of Syria and Anatolia, and the political stability offered by Arsacid protection was, in most decades, better than anything Rome could guarantee along the Egyptian coast.

Trajan's invasion of 114-117 CE is best understood not as a war of glory or frontier security but as a commercial raid on an unprecedented scale. The Roman emperor marched down the Euphrates, took Ctesiphon, and pushed on to the Persian Gulf itself. Cassius Dio records him standing on the shore at Charax, watching a ship depart for India, and lamenting that he was too old to follow Alexander further. The lament is touching, but the strategy was cold. Trajan wanted Characene. He wanted the customs revenue of the Gulf ports. He wanted to splice his empire directly into the Indian trade without paying the Parthian cut.

He did not get it. The conquered provinces revolted behind him, Jewish uprisings broke out across the eastern Mediterranean, and Trajan died on the way home. His successor Hadrian pulled back to the Euphrates and wrote off the experiment. Characene returned to Arsacid orbit, and the silver kept flowing east through channels the Parthians controlled.

What the episode demonstrated was the value of the prize. An emperor of Trajan's ability, at the height of Roman power, had been willing to bet everything on breaking the Parthian monopoly. And he had failed.

Luxury, Coinage, and the Economy of Prestige

Trade on this scale required money, and the Parthians minted a great deal of it. Arsacid silver drachms, struck at Ecbatana and Seleucia and a handful of other mints, were the workhorse currency of the eastern trade for three centuries. They were good silver, reliably weighed, and recognizable at a glance: the obverse showed the reigning king in a distinctive soft cap or diadem, the reverse a seated archer - a reference to the founder Arsaces and to the military identity of the dynasty. Chinese hoards have yielded Parthian coins. So have sites in India, the Caucasus, and the Arabian peninsula.

The tetradrachms struck at Seleucia, heavier coins meant for larger transactions, carried Greek legends and elaborate portraiture that borrowed freely from Hellenistic models. This was deliberate. The Parthians wanted Greek-speaking merchants to feel at home with their money, and they knew that a coin was, among other things, a piece of propaganda. The king's face on every drachm reminded every user whose roads he was using.

Beyond coinage, the Parthian economy ran on what can only be called prestige consumption. The court and the noble families demanded goods that announced status: gold belts and sword fittings, silver-gilt rhytons shaped like animal heads, fine textiles shot through with gold thread, carved gems, imported glass. Archaeology at Nisa, the dynastic sanctuary, has turned up ivory rhytons of astonishing quality, carved with classical mythological scenes - plainly the work of Greek craftsmen working for Iranian patrons. At Hatra and Palmyra, the merchant elite commissioned statues showing themselves in heavy embroidered trousers and tunics whose patterns can still be traced in the stone.

This was not mere vanity. In a society without modern banking, wealth had to be visible to function as power. A noble who could dress his retinue in silk, feast his allies from silver vessels, and give gifts of gold to visiting envoys was broadcasting a message that translated directly into political influence. Trade brought the materials for that broadcast, and the Arsacid court calibrated its tolerance of merchants accordingly. Caravan cities like Palmyra, technically inside the Roman sphere but economically bound to the Parthian routes, were allowed extraordinary autonomy because they were useful.

There was also a darker side to the prestige economy. Concentrating luxury at the top required taxation at the bottom, and the rural population of the Parthian empire - Iranian peasants, Mesopotamian farmers, Central Asian herders - bore loads we can only guess at. The sources are almost entirely silent about them. We see the silk and the silver and the ivory. We see the caravans. We do not see the villagers whose grain fed the caravan drivers and whose labor built the roads.

What the Romans Paid For Silk

On the Roman side, the reaction to the eastern trade was a century-long moral panic about money. Pliny the Elder, writing in the 70s CE, put a number on it that later writers repeated with horror: Rome was losing a hundred million sesterces a year to India, China, and Arabia combined, of which at least fifty-five million went to India alone. The figures cannot be verified, but the direction of travel was undoubtedly right. Roman silver coins have been found by the thousands in southern Indian hoards, often still in mint condition, apparently valued for their metal rather than spent as currency.

What, exactly, were the Romans buying? Silk was the notorious item, but pepper and other spices probably accounted for more of the bill. A Roman cookbook attributed to Apicius calls for pepper in almost every savory recipe. Frankincense and myrrh burned in every temple and at every funeral; the demand was structural, not fashionable. Indian cotton, Chinese lacquer, Arabian pearls, African ivory - each had its market, and together they represented a permanent drain of precious metal from west to east.

Silk became the symbol of the whole anxiety because it was both expensive and morally suspect. Senator Seneca complained that silk garments hid nothing and revealed everything; he called them "wretched flocks of maids" labored so that "the adulteress may be visible through her dress." The Senate tried, more than once, to ban men from wearing silk. The bans failed. By the second century, silk was being unraveled in Syrian workshops and rewoven into lighter, looser Roman fabrics - an early example of an import being adapted to local taste, at the cost of yet more outflowing silver.

The Parthians took their cut at every stage. A Chinese bolt of silk that cost, say, a few hundred Han cash at the loom might sell for its weight in gold by the time it reached a Roman market. Modern estimates suggest the price could multiply a hundredfold along the route. Not all of that increase went into Parthian pockets - transport, losses, and intermediate merchants all took their share - but a substantial fraction did. Customs at the Euphrates crossing, tolls at the mountain passes, harbor dues at Charax, and the simple profit of being the seller to the final buyer all added up.

This is the arithmetic that made Trajan march east, and that made his successors pull back. Rome could not militarily digest the Parthian heartland, and a broken middleman was worse than a greedy one. Better to pay the tolls and grumble. The grumbling produced some excellent literature. It did not produce a policy.

Key Figures & Events

Zhang Qian opened the conversation between Han China and the west through two missions beginning in 138 and 119 BCE, bringing back the first concrete knowledge of Parthia - "Anxi" in Chinese - and setting the silk trade in motion. **Emperor Wu**, his patron, turned that knowledge into a sustained Han policy of western engagement.

Isidore of Charax, writing in the first century BCE, produced in *Parthian Stations* the closest thing we have to a road atlas of the Arsacid empire, listing every staging post from the Euphrates to the Indian frontier. **Mithridates II** likely received the first Han ambassadors and fixed the Parthian place in the new trading order.

Trajan's eastern campaign of 114-117 CE was the most serious Roman attempt to seize the Parthian trade apparatus by force; it reached the Persian Gulf and collapsed almost immediately, confirming that the Arsacid middleman position could not be dislodged.

Analysis

Empires are usually remembered for what they built or conquered. The Parthians are best remembered for what they routed. Their genius was not architectural or literary but logistical: they held a corridor, and they kept it working. The silk that clothed Roman matrons and the pepper that seasoned Roman dinners crossed that corridor, and the taxes they paid at every stage built Parthian palaces at Ctesiphon and Hatra, funded the cataphract armies that humiliated Crassus and Antony, and paid the salaries of the scribes who registered their passage.

This quiet, commercial basis of Arsacid power explains much that would otherwise puzzle us. It explains why the Parthians tolerated so much local autonomy - Characene, Palmyra, the Greek cities - when those arrangements kept the trade flowing. It explains why Chinese and Roman sources, so hostile to each other's cultures, agree that the middle kingdom of Anxi was rich beyond ordinary measure. It explains why Rome, for all its military superiority in set-piece battles, could never convert victory into lasting gain east of the Euphrates: you cannot occupy a trade network, you can only join it or tax it.

All of this hints at something larger about ancient world history. The integration of Eurasia, usually credited to Mongols a thousand years later or to Europeans a millennium after that, was in practical terms already substantial by 100 CE. A Chinese silk, an Indian pepper, a Roman silver coin, and a Parthian customs stamp could cohabit in the same saddlebag. The world was already stitched together. The Arsacids held the needle.

Quick Summary

- The Parthian empire straddled the only practical overland route between China and the Mediterranean, allowing the Arsacids to tax commerce at every stage.
- Isidore of Charax's *Parthian Stations* preserves a detailed itinerary of the trunk road from the Euphrates to India.
- Zhang Qian's missions (138 and 119 BCE) opened direct Han Chinese contact with "Anxi" - the Parthian realm - and launched regular silk exports westward.
- A later Han envoy, Gan Ying, was talked out of sailing to Rome by Parthian sailors in 97 CE; the Arsacids deliberately prevented direct Sino-Roman contact.
- Characene, at the head of the Persian Gulf, served as the key maritime hub linking Parthia to the Indian Ocean trade.
- Trajan's invasion of 114-117 CE was essentially a commercial raid aimed at seizing these revenues; it failed within three years.
- Roman writers like Pliny estimated annual losses of a hundred million sesterces to the eastern trade, much of it ending up as silver hoards in India and beyond.

- Parthian silver drachms, reliable and widely accepted, became the workhorse currency of long-distance Asian commerce.

The Arsacids left no epic poetry, no monumental history, and very few surviving buildings of their own. What they left were coins, caravan stations, and customs records - the unromantic infrastructure of a working economy that briefly made the known world smaller. For five hundred years, the price of silk in a Roman market and the supply of glass in a Chinese tomb were both, in the end, set by decisions made in Ctesiphon. That is a kind of power historians have been slow to recognize, and slower still to respect. The Parthians understood it perfectly. They counted it in drachms.

The caravans carried more than silk and glass. They carried priests, preachers, scrolls, and ideas, and the Arsacid kings who taxed the trade also had to decide what to do with the beliefs traveling alongside it. An empire stretched across so many peoples could not afford a state creed, and the Parthians, to their credit, rarely tried to impose one. The result was a religious landscape of extraordinary variety, held together by a light royal hand. What the Arsacids did, and did not do, with the gods deserves a closer look.

Chapter 9:

Gods of the Arsacids

On a silver drachm struck in the first century CE, the Arsacid king gazes out in profile, bearded and diademed, while the reverse shows a seated archer - a Greek-style image of a distinctly Iranian hero. The same king who paid craftsmen to carve Greek letters around his portrait also kept sacred fires burning in the old Iranian manner, tolerated rabbis teaching Torah in Babylonia, and watched, perhaps with curiosity, as merchants along the Euphrates began whispering about a crucified Galilean.

Few empires have ever hosted so many faiths at once, and fewer still have done so with such apparent indifference to orthodoxy. For nearly five centuries, from the first horsemen of Arsaces to the final stand of Ardavan V in 224 CE, the Parthian realm functioned as a vast religious crossroads. Zoroastrian priests tended fires on the Iranian plateau. Greek colonists offered wine to Apollo in Seleucia. Jewish exilarchs presided over ancient communities along the Tigris. Armenian kings - Arsacid cousins, as it happened - learned to fuse Iranian and Anatolian gods into a single pantheon. And from the first century onward, Christian missionaries found a surprisingly hospitable hearing east of the Roman frontier. No Parthian king demanded that his subjects worship as he did. That monopolistic impulse would arrive only with the Sassanians who overthrew them. Understanding how the Arsacids ruled over this plurality - and why they declined to flatten it - is to understand what made their empire distinct.

Zoroastrianism Under the Arsacids

The Arsacids were Iranians, and the faith of their ancestors was the faith of Zarathustra. Fire, purity, the cosmic struggle between the good creator Ahura Mazda and the lie-spirit Ahriman - these were the inherited furniture of their religious world. Yet it would be a mistake to imagine the Parthian court as a theocracy in miniature.

Zoroastrianism under the Arsacids was a lived tradition rather than an imposed creed. There was no state church, no caste of inquisitors, no authorized scripture enforced from the capital. The Avesta, the sacred corpus, circulated orally among priestly families, the magi, who preserved hymns and rituals that had been old already when Cyrus the Great ruled. These magi served as advisors, astrologers, judges in matters of inheritance and pollution, and guardians of the royal fires. But they did not run the empire.

What the Arsacids did do, quietly and consistently, was behave like Zoroastrian kings. They practiced khvaetvadatha, close-kin marriage, a custom that horrified Greek and Roman observers but which Iranian tradition regarded as meritorious, a means of preserving the purity of noble bloodlines. They swore oaths by Mithra, the god of covenants, whose name appears again and again in Parthian royal nomenclature. They endowed fire temples whose ashes, archaeologists have found, were kept burning for generations at sites like Takht-e Soleyman.

The reign of Vologases I, in the middle of the first century CE, marks a subtle turning point. Ancient tradition - preserved much later in Sassanian-era Zoroastrian texts - credits him with commissioning the first written collection of the Avesta, gathering scattered hymns and rulings that had survived the Hellenistic centuries in fragmentary form. Whether Vologases personally ordered such a project or whether later priests retrojected their own work onto a sympathetic king, the story captures something real. Under his rule, Iranian elements of the Parthian identity grew more visible. Coins shifted from Greek to Aramaic script. Royal titulature emphasized ancestral legitimacy. The veneer of Hellenism, so prominent on early Arsacid drachms, began to thin.

Nowhere was the Zoroastrian dimension of Arsacid rule more consequential than in Armenia. When Vologases installed his brother Tiridates on the Armenian throne in the 60s CE - a settlement grudgingly accepted by Nero after a long war - he was not merely planting a Parthian prince in a client kingdom. He was exporting a branch of the Arsacid house that would carry Iranian religion deep into the Caucasus. Tiridates, according to Pliny, traveled to Rome to receive his crown but refused to sail, unwilling to pollute the sea, a Zoroastrian scruple that bemused his hosts. In Armenia the royal dynasty he founded built fire temples, honored Mithra and Anahita under local names, and planted a form of Iranian paganism so deep that when Armenia eventually converted to Christianity in the early fourth century, the new religion had to absorb and repurpose an enormous stock of Zoroastrian vocabulary.

Yet even as Iranian religion grew more prominent, the Arsacids declined to make it exclusive. Their subjects worshipped as they pleased. The decision to leave the empire religiously plural was not weakness. It was policy.

Greek Gods, Local Gods, Shared Gods

Walk into the ruins of Seleucia-on-the-Tigris, the great commercial city the Parthians inherited from Alexander's successors, and you walk into a religious thicket. Clay figurines of Heracles sit beside images of Nergal, the old Mesopotamian god of the underworld. Greek altars stand near Babylonian shrines. Aramaic dedications mingle with Greek inscriptions. No single deity presided. Everyone presided.

The Arsacids inherited this Hellenistic-Mesopotamian amalgam and chose not to disrupt it. Their own coins proudly styled them *Philhellene*, friend of the Greeks, a title that served double duty as reassurance to urban populations and as a declaration that Parthian kingship need not be ethnically narrow. Apollo seated on the omphalos remained a standard reverse image on their silver for over a century. In the temples of Babylonia, cuneiform astronomical diaries continued to be compiled into the first century BCE, patronized or at least tolerated by a court that saw no reason to silence the world's oldest scribal tradition.

Out on the middle Euphrates, at the caravan city of Dura-Europos, the Parthians presided over one of the most extraordinary religious collages in the ancient world. In a single town, worshippers maintained shrines to Zeus and Artemis, to the Palmyrene gods Bel and Yarhibol, to Adonis and Atargatis, and - in time - to the Jewish God and the Christian Christ. Dura's famous synagogue, with its astonishing cycle of biblical frescoes, and its tiny Christian house church, the earliest yet excavated anywhere, both took shape under Parthian or Parthian-influenced rule before the Romans seized the town. The permission to build such spaces, in such proximity, was not accidental. It was the atmosphere of the empire.

Farther east, on the frontier with India, a different kind of blending flourished. At Hatra, an Arab-Parthian city in the northern Mesopotamian steppe, the sun god Shamash was honored as Maran, "Our Lord," and portrayed with a Greek eagle at his side. The kings of Hatra styled themselves servants of Shamash while wearing Parthian dress and swearing by Parthian overlords. At Commagene, just before its absorption into Rome, the king Antiochus I had erected colossal statues at Nemrut Dagh pairing Zeus with Oromasdes (Ahura Mazda), Apollo with Mithras, Heracles with Artagnes (Verethragna). This theological equation - Greek god equals Iranian god equals local god - was the common currency of the Parthian world.

A plural religious field is a stable one. When every major constituency has a temple, none has a grievance. When the king patronizes all, none can claim him exclusively. Out of this practical wisdom grew one of antiquity's most durable experiments in coexistence.

The Jewish Exilarchate in Babylonia

The Jews of Babylonia were older than the Arsacids by half a millennium. Their ancestors had been marched east by Nebuchadnezzar in 586 BCE, settled along the canals of the Tigris and Euphrates, and had stubbornly remained there when Cyrus permitted them to return to Jerusalem. By the time the Parthians took the region, the community had roots sunk so deep they were indistinguishable from the soil. They spoke Aramaic, farmed the alluvial plain, traded in Seleucia and Ctesiphon, and produced scholars whose reputation was already spreading back to Judaea.

Under the Arsacids, this ancient diaspora entered a golden age. The kings of Parthia granted the Jewish community an unusual form of internal self-government, headed by an official known as the Exilarch - in Aramaic the Resh Galuta, "Head of the Exile." The Exilarch was claimed, according to later tradition, to descend from the Davidic line through King Jehoiachin, the last Judean monarch to be exiled to Babylon. Whether or not the genealogy was historical, the institution was real. The Exilarch collected taxes, appointed judges, represented the community at court, and held a rank at royal functions that no Jewish leader anywhere else in the world possessed.

For the Arsacids, this arrangement was efficient. A populous, wealthy, and historically restive community could be governed through its own notables rather than through Parthian officials who would not speak the language or understand the law. For the Jews, the arrangement was transformative. Babylonia became a center of religious scholarship rivalling - and eventually surpassing - the academies of the Holy Land. The schools of Nehardea and, later, Sura and Pumbedita, founded in the closing Parthian centuries, would in time produce the Babylonian Talmud, the text that shaped Judaism for the next two thousand years.

Political gratitude ran deep. When the Roman general Crassus looted the Temple treasury in 54 BCE on his way to his catastrophic defeat at Carrhae, Babylonian Jews cheered the Parthian victory. When Judaea rose against Rome in the great revolt of 66 CE, and again in the Bar Kokhba revolt of 132-135, Jewish communities in the east watched and sometimes hoped for Parthian intervention. It rarely came in the form rebels wanted, but the cultural alignment was unmistakable. Rome was the destroyer of the Temple; Parthia was the protector of the exile.

A single vivid episode captures the unusual place of the Jewish community. In the early first century CE, two brothers named Anilaeus and Asinaeus, Jews from Nehardea, carved out a small brigand principality in the marshes of southern Mesopotamia. For roughly fifteen years they ruled as warlords, collecting tolls, fighting Parthian nobles, and negotiating directly with King Artabanus II, who preferred to recognize their autonomy rather than destroy them. Only when their regime collapsed through internal quarrels did the experiment end. That a pair of Jewish outlaws could become, however briefly, functional partners of the Parthian crown tells us a great deal about the flexibility of Arsacid governance.

By the time the Sassanians replaced the Arsacids in 224 CE, the Babylonian Jewish community was the most populous, prosperous, and learned in the world. It owed much of that stature to four centuries of Parthian forbearance.

Christianity Reaches Mesopotamia

Sometime in the first century CE, along the caravan routes that ran from Antioch to the Tigris, the new faith arrived. It came first, almost certainly, through the existing Jewish communities - missionaries who spoke Aramaic to Aramaic-speaking synagogues and found ready audiences among Gentile sympathizers on the fringes. By the second century, Christian congregations existed at Edessa, Arbela, and in the suburbs of Ctesiphon itself.

Edessa, a small kingdom straddling the Roman-Parthian frontier, occupies a particular place in this story. Its ruling dynasty, the Abgarids, would later be remembered in Christian legend as the first royal house in the world to convert, allegedly through correspondence between King Abgar V and Jesus himself. The legend is almost certainly fictional, but it rests on a genuine historical core: by the late second century, Edessa had a substantial Christian community and a king, Abgar VIII, who was at the very least sympathetic. From Edessa, Syriac Christianity - a distinctive form of the faith conducted in a dialect of Aramaic - spread east across Parthian territory.

The apostolic traditions of the Eastern Church trace these missions to specific figures. Thomas, according to the Syriac Acts of Thomas, evangelized Parthia and India. Addai and his disciple Mari, hazier figures historically, are credited with founding the churches of Mesopotamia. What these traditions preserve, beneath their layers of embellishment, is the memory that Christianity arrived in the Parthian east very early, perhaps as early as it reached Rome, and through different channels.

The critical point is that it could arrive at all. Under the Roman emperors, Christians suffered periodic persecution - sporadic, localized, but real. Under the Arsacids, there is no record of any organized effort to suppress the new religion. Christian communities worshipped freely, built small churches like the one excavated at Dura-Europos, translated their scriptures into Syriac, and produced theologians such as Tatian and, later, Bardaisan, whose hymns and cosmological speculations drew on the full intellectual wealth of the Parthian world.

The contrast with what followed is stark. When the Sassanians came to power and elevated Zoroastrianism to the status of a state religion, the toleration that Christians had enjoyed for nearly two centuries evaporated. The great persecutions of the fourth century - under Shapur II - would reduce whole communities to martyrs. In retrospect, the Parthian era would look, to Eastern Christians, like a lost age of peace.

The Cult of the King

Above all the priests and rabbis and bishops stood the king himself, and around the Arsacid monarch coalesced a cult of his own.

Parthian kings styled themselves with titles that make the point unmistakable. *Basileus Basileon*, King of Kings, was their standard Greek legend, inherited from the Achaemenids who had first made the phrase famous. On their coins they appeared diademed in the Hellenistic fashion but also, increasingly, wearing the tall Iranian tiara. Some used the Greek epithet *Theopator*, "whose father is a god," or *Epiphanes*, "god manifest." Whether these titles represented sincere theological claims or royal bombast is a question as old as Hellenistic kingship itself, and the honest answer is probably both at once.

The Arsacids traced their descent, at least in official propaganda, back to the Achaemenid Artaxerxes II. This claim, almost certainly invented, served a religious as well as a political purpose. It bound the ruling house to the great Iranian kings of the past, to the guardians of Ahura Mazda's order on earth, and to a royal tradition in which the monarch was not merely a ruler but a pivot in the cosmic struggle between truth and the lie. The king's justice kept the fires burning. The king's victories pushed back the forces of chaos. The king's personal purity - maintained through ritual, through marriage, through observance - mattered to the whole realm.

Royal investiture took place at Asaak, in the heartland of Parthia, where a sacred fire was said to have been kindled by Arsaces himself and tended in unbroken succession. To be crowned there was to step into a chain of legitimacy that stretched back to the founding of the dynasty. Coins from various reigns show kings receiving the diadem from a goddess - sometimes identified as Tyche, sometimes as Anahita, the Iranian goddess of waters and sovereignty. The ambiguity was deliberate. A Greek subject saw Fortune crowning her favorite. An Iranian subject saw the ancient Lady of the Waters confirming her chosen king. Both were right.

Dynastic ritual extended to death as well as life. The tombs of the Arsacids at Nisa, in modern Turkmenistan, housed royal portraits and, almost certainly, rituals of ancestor veneration that drew on both Iranian and Hellenistic precedents. The ivory rhytons discovered there - drinking horns carved with mythological scenes - suggest ceremonial banquets in which the living kings communed, in some fashion, with the dead ones.

What the cult of the king provided, above all, was a unifying focus in an empire that otherwise lacked one. A Jew in Nehardea and a Greek in Seleucia and a Zoroastrian magus in Ecbatana shared almost nothing religiously. But they all owed allegiance to the King of Kings, and they all could, in their own idiom, acknowledge his sacred standing. Arsacid theology, such as it was, worked by addition rather than subtraction.

Analysis

The religious policy of the Parthian Empire - if such a deliberate thing existed - was essentially one of strategic restraint. The Arsacids were Zoroastrian by inheritance, conviction, and ritual practice. They could have attempted, as the Sassanians later would, to impose their ancestral faith on every subject. They did not. Instead they ruled a patchwork of communities, each with its own gods, clergy, and courts, and they bound the whole together through a combination of royal charisma, practical toleration, and careful patronage.

The results were remarkable. Babylonian Judaism flourished as it had not flourished anywhere else. Syriac Christianity took root in the east before Constantine had ever been imagined. Greek cities continued to function as Greek cities, two centuries after Alexander. Iranian religion spread peacefully into Armenia. At the center of it all, the Arsacid king held court as a figure who could plausibly be addressed in any of half a dozen religious vocabularies.

When the Sassanians swept this system away in 224 CE, they replaced it with something more ideologically coherent and, as it turned out, more fragile. A state Zoroastrianism empowered priests, clarified doctrine, and produced the first fixed Avesta. It also produced persecution, internal dissent, and eventually the rapid collapse of Iranian religion before the Arab conquest four centuries later. The Arsacid method - let everyone pray as they please, and collect the taxes - looks in hindsight less like tolerance and more like prudent statecraft. It held an empire together for nearly half a millennium.

Quick Summary

- The Arsacids were Zoroastrian by inheritance but never established a state church; religious orthodoxy was not an Arsacid concern.
- Vologases I (reigned c. 51-78 CE) is associated with a strengthening of Iranian religious identity and, in later tradition, with an early effort to collect the Avesta.
- Greek, Mesopotamian, and Iranian gods coexisted and were often identified with one another, especially at sites like Dura-Europos, Hatra, and Commagene.
- The Jewish community of Babylonia enjoyed self-government under the Exilarch and flourished into the most important center of Jewish learning in the world.
- Christianity reached the Parthian east in the first and second centuries CE through Jewish networks and trade routes, with Edessa emerging as a major early center.
- Parthian kings styled themselves King of Kings, claimed Achaemenid descent, and combined Greek and Iranian sacral imagery on their coinage.

- Sacred fires at Asaak and dynastic rituals at Nisa reinforced the king's role as a cosmic as well as political figure.
- The Sassanian replacement of Arsacid pluralism with state Zoroastrianism after 224 CE ended an exceptional era of religious coexistence.

The gods of the Arsacids were many, and their king ruled over all of them without belonging exclusively to any. It was an unusual arrangement - too unusual, perhaps, to last. But for five centuries, in the quiet spaces between Rome's censorious piety and the dogmatic certainties that would follow, the Parthians demonstrated that an empire could be held together by something other than a single creed. The memory of that achievement lingered in the Jewish academies of Babylonia, in the Syriac hymns of the eastern churches, and in the fire temples of Armenia long after the last Arsacid had fallen. It is one of the quieter legacies of the forgotten empire, and one of the most generous.

Tolerating many gods was part of a larger habit of mind. The Arsacids were equally unwilling to choose between the Greek and Iranian worlds they had inherited, and the result was a civilization that struck Greek coins with Iranian titles, performed Euripides at Iranian courts, and carved Hellenistic gods into distinctly Persian reliefs. The religious pluralism of the empire was one face of a deeper cultural pluralism, one that has puzzled observers from the Sasanians onward. The synthesis itself, and its long shadow on later Iran, is worth examining on its own terms.

Chapter 10:

Greek Souls, Iranian Bones - The Parthian Cultural Synthesis

In 53 BCE, somewhere in the royal halls of Armenia, an actor held up the freshly severed head of the Roman general Marcus Licinius Crassus and declaimed verses from a four-century-old Greek tragedy. The audience applauded. The king of kings smiled. And somewhere in that grisly, erudite moment lies the entire puzzle of Parthian civilization.

The Arsacid dynasty ruled an empire that stretched from the Euphrates to the Hindu Kush for nearly five centuries, and in all that time its kings could not quite decide - or perhaps refused to decide - what kind of rulers they wished to be. They minted coins in Greek and called themselves friends of the Hellenes. They revived Iranian royal rituals their Achaemenid ancestors would have recognized. They patronized Athenian drama and Zoroastrian priests in the same week. Out of this sustained refusal to choose emerged something genuinely new: a hybrid civilization that borrowed freely, translated constantly, and belonged entirely to neither the Greek nor the Iranian world it straddled. For generations, scholars dismissed Parthian culture as derivative, a muddled echo of better civilizations on either side. That verdict is being overturned. What the Arsacids built was not confusion. It was synthesis - deliberate, distinctive, and astonishingly durable.

The Philhellene Coinage

Pick up a Parthian silver drachm - any of the thousands that survive in museum trays from Tehran to London - and you hold a small political argument in your hand. On the obverse, a bearded king in profile, often wearing the soft Iranian tiara or a jewel-set diadem. On the reverse, an archer seated on a throne, bow extended: an unmistakable image of Iranian kingship drawn from the steppe heritage of the Parni. And around that archer, running in neat Greek letters, the title: *Basileos Basileon*, King of Kings, followed very often by the word *Philhellenos* - Lover of the Greeks.

The pairing is startling once you notice it. An Iranian horse-archer captioned in the language of Plato. The coinage was not an accident of engraving tradition. Mithridates I, who conquered Media and Babylonia in the 140s BCE and transformed a tribal kingdom into an empire, made the choice deliberately. His new subjects in Mesopotamia and the Iranian plateau included hundreds of Greek and Macedonian cities planted by Alexander and the Seleucids. Seleucia-on-the-Tigris alone housed tens of thousands of Greek speakers. A king who wanted their taxes and their loyalty needed to speak their visual language.

So Mithridates and his successors did. Their portraits adopted the Hellenistic convention of the royal profile, the diadem borrowed from Alexander, the clean-shaven youthful idealism of early Seleucid coinage - though the Arsacids quickly reintroduced the beard, an Iranian marker of masculine dignity that Greek rulers had abandoned. The Greek inscriptions grew longer and more elaborate over generations, accumulating epithets: *Epiphanes* (God Manifest), *Euergetes* (Benefactor), *Dikaios* (the Just). These were the titles of Seleucid kings, now claimed by the men who had driven the Seleucids out.

There is something almost cheeky in the appropriation. The Arsacids were not flattering Greek culture from a position of weakness. They had defeated the greatest Hellenistic power of the age. Yet they presented themselves to their new subjects not as conquerors imposing alien rule but as legitimate inheritors of the Alexandrian project, civilized kings who happened to be Iranian. *Philhellenos* was a diplomatic gesture and a cultural claim at once.

The claim held for nearly two centuries on the coins, even as the political reality beneath shifted. Only in the first century CE, under Vologases I and his successors, did the Greek begin to corrupt, letters growing garbled as the die-cutters themselves lost fluency. By then the Parthian language was appearing alongside it, tentatively at first, then with growing confidence. The coinage recorded in miniature the long swing of a civilization recovering its Iranian voice without ever entirely abandoning its Greek one. The archer stayed on the throne throughout.

Greek Theater in Parthian Territory

The story of Crassus's head deserves to be told properly, because it is one of those small episodes in which an entire civilization shows itself. Plutarch preserved it, and though he wrote a century and a half later, the details have the ring of something remembered rather than invented.

In May of 53 BCE, Crassus - triumvir, plutocrat, and the richest man in Rome - led seven legions across the Euphrates in search of glory. He found catastrophe instead. At Carrhae, the Parthian general Surena destroyed his army with mounted archers and armored lancers, killing some twenty thousand Romans and capturing ten thousand more. Crassus himself died in the aftermath, his head and hand cut off and dispatched as trophies to the Parthian king Orodes II.

Orodes was at that moment in Armenia, celebrating a diplomatic triumph. He had married his son Pacorus to the sister of the Armenian king Artavasdes II, and the two courts were entertaining themselves with a performance of Euripides's *Bacchae*. Both kings spoke Greek fluently. Artavasdes wrote Greek tragedies of his own, now lost. They were watching a play more than four centuries old, composed in Athens during the Peloponnesian War, about the god Dionysus and the terrible vengeance he takes on the Theban king Pentheus - whose mother, in a Bacchic frenzy, tears off her son's head and carries it onstage, thinking it the head of a lion.

The messenger with Crassus's head arrived mid-performance. The leading actor, a man named Jason of Tralles, seized his moment. He set aside the prop head he had been carrying, took up the actual head of the Roman general, and delivered the climactic lines of Agave over the real object: *We bring from the mountain a tendril fresh-cut to the palace, a wonderful prey.* The audience, Plutarch tells us, roared with delight.

One can recoil from the cruelty and still recognize what the scene reveals. Here were the kings of Parthia and Armenia, on the eastern edge of the Hellenistic world, drawing on a Greek theatrical tradition so thoroughly naturalized among them that an improvising actor could instantly match a Roman head to an Athenian metaphor. The court understood the allusion. The joke worked because everyone in the hall knew the play by heart.

Greek theaters have been excavated across former Parthian territory, from Seleucia to Babylon to the cities of the Iranian plateau. The Arsacid court maintained Greek actors and musicians. Royal correspondence in Greek circulated through the chancelleries of the Near East for generations after Rome had subdued the Mediterranean. A Parthian prince educated at court in the first century BCE would have known his Euripides as surely as a Roman aristocrat knew his Homer.

What the Crassus episode shows is not simply cultural veneer but fluency - the kind that permits improvisation under pressure. Greek had become one of the languages in which Parthian power expressed itself, and Greek drama one of the stages on which Parthian victory could be celebrated. That it was celebrated in this particular way - savage content inside elegant form - is perhaps the most Parthian thing about the whole affair.

The Return of Aramaic and Parthian as Written Languages

For roughly two centuries after Alexander, Greek was the prestige language of everything east of the Aegean that mattered. Royal decrees, tax receipts, tomb inscriptions, philosophical treatises, love poems - Greek handled them all. The Iranian languages of the Achaemenid past survived in speech but almost vanished from the written record. Under the Seleucids, literate business happened in Greek or it did not happen at all.

The Parthians reversed this, slowly and without ever quite saying so. The first signs appear in Aramaic, the old administrative language of the Achaemenid empire, which had never entirely died out in Mesopotamia and the Levant. Parthian scribes revived it for everyday bureaucratic use: tax records, ostraca, the thousands of small business documents excavated at Nisa, the early Parthian capital in what is now Turkmenistan. The Nisa ostraca, written in Aramaic script but often reflecting Parthian vocabulary and grammar beneath, date to the first century BCE and capture the moment when an Iranian administration began to think in Iranian again.

From Aramaic the path led to something stranger and more consequential: the development of written Parthian itself. Scribes took the Aramaic alphabet and adapted it to record their own Middle Iranian language. They also developed a peculiar system of *heterograms* - Aramaic words written on the page but read aloud in Parthian. A scribe would write the Aramaic word for king, *MLK*, but the reader would pronounce it *shah*. The Aramaic was a kind of ideogram, a visual shorthand for an Iranian meaning. This halfway house between two languages became standard and survived, remarkably, into the Sasanian period and beyond. Middle Persian scribes were still writing Aramaic heterograms in the seventh century CE, nearly a thousand years after the practice began.

By the reign of Vologases I in the mid-first century CE, the shift had become political. Vologases issued coins with Parthian legends alongside the Greek. He is credited by later Zoroastrian tradition - perhaps accurately, perhaps legendarily - with beginning the collection of the scattered oral texts of the Avesta, the sacred scriptures of Zoroastrianism, which had been transmitted from memory for centuries. Whether or not Vologases personally sponsored the work, a cultural program was clearly under way: the deliberate reclamation of Iranian religious and linguistic heritage after centuries of Hellenistic dominance.

None of this came at the cost of Greek, which continued to appear on coins and in elite contexts into the second century CE. The Parthian method was layering, not replacement. A royal document might exist in Greek for the western subjects, in Aramaic for the Mesopotamian bureaucracy, and in Parthian for the Iranian heartland. A single administration used three languages without apparent anxiety.

The cultural consequences ran deep. When the Sasanians overthrew the last Arsacid in 224 CE and set about constructing a self-consciously Iranian empire, they inherited a functioning written Iranian language, a living Zoroastrian tradition, and a scribal culture that could handle the demands of imperial administration without reaching for Greek. The Sasanians often get credit for the Iranian revival. Much of the work was already done. The Parthians, for all their philhellenism, had quietly prepared the ground on which a Persian empire could stand again.

Art: Frontality, Costume, and the Parthian Style

Walk into the gallery of Parthian sculpture at any major museum and you will meet faces that look straight back at you. This is the single most discussed feature of Parthian art: frontality. Where Greek sculpture prefers the three-quarter view, the turned head, the implied motion through space, Parthian figures face directly outward. Kings, gods, worshippers, warriors - they confront the viewer head-on, eyes wide, symmetrical and still.

Art historians once treated this as evidence of decline, a loss of Greek skill. The modern view is nearly opposite. Frontality was a choice, not a failure, and it carried meaning. A frontal figure is a figure in relation to the viewer - a god receiving a prayer, a king receiving homage, a donor presenting himself to the sacred. The Parthians were not trying to render narrative motion in the Greek manner. They were rendering encounter. The style spread from the Parthian realm throughout the Near East and shaped early Christian, Byzantine, and Sasanian art for centuries. Those staring saints in Byzantine mosaics are the great-grandchildren of Parthian princes.

The costume is equally distinctive. Parthian male figures - in sculpture at Hatra, in rock reliefs at Bisotun, in wall paintings at Dura-Europos - wear tunics belted at the waist, long trousers gathered into soft boots, and elaborately draped cloaks. The trousers are crucial. Greeks despised trousers as barbaric; Romans found them outlandish until their own cavalry began wearing them. The Parthians embraced them as practical wear for horsemen and dignified them in royal portraiture. Often shown baggy and richly patterned, with soft boots and belts decorated with roundels, this was a cavalry aristocracy representing itself truthfully: men who lived in the saddle.

The statues from Hatra, the caravan city in the Mesopotamian desert, show the style at its most developed. Local rulers and priests stand in rigid frontality, dressed in the full Parthian costume, hands raised in gestures of prayer or authority. The faces are strongly individualized - these are portraits of specific people - but the bodies follow a common formal code. Jewelry is lavish, beards are carefully curled, every fold of drapery is deliberate. It is not Greek naturalism and it is not Achaemenid monumentality. It is something else, self-possessed and new.

At Dura-Europos on the Euphrates, excavated in the 1920s and 30s, archaeologists uncovered wall paintings in temples, synagogues, and churches that demonstrate how thoroughly the Parthian visual vocabulary had spread. Jewish patriarchs, Palmyrene gods, and Christian saints all appear in the same frontal poses, the same trousered costumes, the same staring eyes. A shared regional style had emerged that cut across religious and ethnic boundaries. It happened to be Parthian.

Greek influence survived, but transformed. Drapery techniques, contrapposto in a few early royal reliefs, the occasional acanthus leaf or

Corinthian capital - these elements appear, absorbed into a different aesthetic logic. Parthian artists were not failed Greeks. They were successful Parthians, working out how to represent an Iranian world to itself in a visual language of their own making. Only in the twentieth century did scholars begin to see the coherence of the result. The older dismissals, which treated anything non-Hellenic as lesser, said more about modern prejudice than about ancient artistry.

The Epic Tradition and Lost Parthian Literature

Almost no Parthian literature survives. This is the single hardest fact to accept about a civilization that ruled for five centuries. No epic, no history, no philosophical treatise, no body of lyric poetry remains intact from the Arsacid period in a Parthian language. What we have are inscriptions, coin legends, administrative documents, and quotations preserved by hostile successors. The rest is gone.

And yet multiple converging indications confirm that a vast literary tradition existed. The Sasanians inherited it. The Islamic historians who later assembled the grand compendia of Iranian legend - above all Firdawsi in the *Shahnameh*, completed around 1010 CE - drew on older Middle Persian compilations that themselves drew on Parthian sources. Many of the heroes who dominate the *Shahnameh* are Parthian in origin: Rostam, the great warrior-champion whose seven labors and tragic killing of his own son Sohrab anchor the epic, belongs to the Sistan cycle, a body of hero-tales that flourished in the eastern Parthian world. The entire *pahlavan* ideal - the armored cavalry champion, loyal to his king, bound by honor - is a Parthian aristocratic ideal transmitted into Persian memory.

How did this literature circulate? Largely by performance. The *gosan*, the minstrel-bard, was a fixture of Parthian court and camp, playing a stringed instrument and singing verse narratives about kings, heroes, battles, and lovers. Armenian sources, written by neighbors who knew the Parthian world intimately, describe the gosans vividly, and the Armenian epic tradition - the cycle of Sasun, the tales of Artashes - is saturated with Parthian material. The minstrel carried the stories that the scribes did not write down, and when the minstrels fell silent the stories passed to other hands, other languages, other forms.

The losses were not accidental. The Sasanians, for political reasons, tended to minimize Parthian achievement in the official histories they sponsored. The centuries of Arsacid rule were compressed, sometimes reduced to a list of petty kings. When Islamic conquest came in the seventh century, much of what survived in Zoroastrian temple libraries was further winnowed. What made it through to the *Shahnameh* did so partly by being absorbed into a Persian frame that obscured its Parthian origins.

Scholars have spent the last century patiently reconstructing what was lost. The Sistan cycle, the Kayanian legends as Parthians shaped them, the love story of Vis and Ramin (preserved in an eleventh-century Persian poem but based on a Parthian original), the traces of Parthian meter and vocabulary in later verse - all of this points to a living literary world as rich as anything in the Mediterranean, now audible only as echo. The Parthians told stories about themselves, in their own language, to audiences that stretched from the Oxus to the Euphrates. Those stories shaped how Iranians would imagine heroism, kingship, and love for the next thousand years. The silence of the surviving record is misleading. Rostam still rides.

Analysis

The easy way to describe Parthian culture is to call it a mixture - Greek plus Iranian, with some Mesopotamian and steppe elements stirred in. The description is accurate and entirely misses the point. Every imperial culture is a mixture. What matters is the chemistry of the blend, the way particular combinations produce particular possibilities.

The Parthians accomplished something unusual: they maintained cultural doubleness for centuries without resolving it. They did not assimilate to Greek civilization, as some expected them to; they did not expel it, as the Sasanians partly would. They held both languages, both visual traditions, both religious vocabularies in play, and they let different audiences receive different versions of the same royal message. A Greek subject in Seleucia saw a philhellene king on his coin. An Iranian noble in Nisa heard a minstrel sing of Arsacid descent from the old Achaemenid line. Both pictures were true, and both were partial.

This pluralism was not weakness. It was the operating principle of an empire that held together wildly different populations without the coercive administrative machinery of Rome or the ideological uniformity of later Sasanian Iran. The cost was the thinness of the written record - a culture that refuses to choose one language for its official memory ends up with fragments in several. The benefit was longevity, and a cultural legacy that outlasted the dynasty itself. Sasanian art inherited Parthian frontality. Persian epic inherited Parthian heroes. Byzantine saints stared out at their worshippers with Parthian eyes.

Quick Summary

- Arsacid coinage combined Iranian imagery (the seated archer, the beard) with Greek inscriptions, including the royal epithet *Philhellenos*, signaling legitimacy to both Greek and Iranian subjects.
- Greek drama was deeply naturalized at Parthian courts; Euripides's *Bacchae* was performed before Orodes II and Artavasdes II in 53 BCE, the occasion of the macabre use of Crassus's severed head as a prop.
- From the first century BCE onward, Aramaic and then written Parthian gradually reasserted themselves as administrative and

eventually royal languages, using Aramaic-derived scripts and heterograms.

- Vologases I is associated with the early collection of Zoroastrian scriptures and the growing prominence of Parthian-language coin legends.
- Parthian art developed a distinctive style characterized by frontality, elaborate cavalry costume including trousers, and strong individual portraiture, influencing later Sasanian, Byzantine, and early Christian art.
- Little Parthian literature survives directly, but its epic tradition - preserved by minstrels called gosans - fed Armenian epic and Firdawsi's *Shahnameh*, including the hero Rostam and the Sistan cycle.
- The Parthian cultural model was layered rather than unified, allowing Greek and Iranian traditions to coexist for centuries without resolution.

When the last Arsacid fell in 224 CE, Ardashir and his Sasanian successors claimed to be restoring a pure Iranian tradition after centuries of foreign contamination. The claim was useful politics and bad history. What the Sasanians inherited - their scribal system, their epic heroes, their frontal art, their cavalry aristocracy, their functioning Zoroastrian priesthood - had been shaped decisively by the five centuries of Arsacid rule they preferred to forget. The Parthians had done the quiet, unglamorous work of keeping an Iranian civilization alive inside a Hellenistic shell, then slowly turning the shell inside out. By the time anyone noticed, the synthesis was complete, and much of what we now think of as classical Persian culture was already Parthian in its bones.

A civilization that could hold Greek and Iranian elements in productive tension was, in some sense, built for frontiers. Nowhere was that gift more tested than in the mountainous kingdom wedged between Ctesiphon and the Euphrates, where Parthian and Roman ambitions met and refused to resolve.

Armenia was not simply a buffer. It was a laboratory in which the Arsacid talent for ruling through other rulers was put to its hardest test, against an opponent equally determined and equally unable to finish the job. The Armenian question shaped both empires for three centuries.

Chapter 11:

The Armenian Question

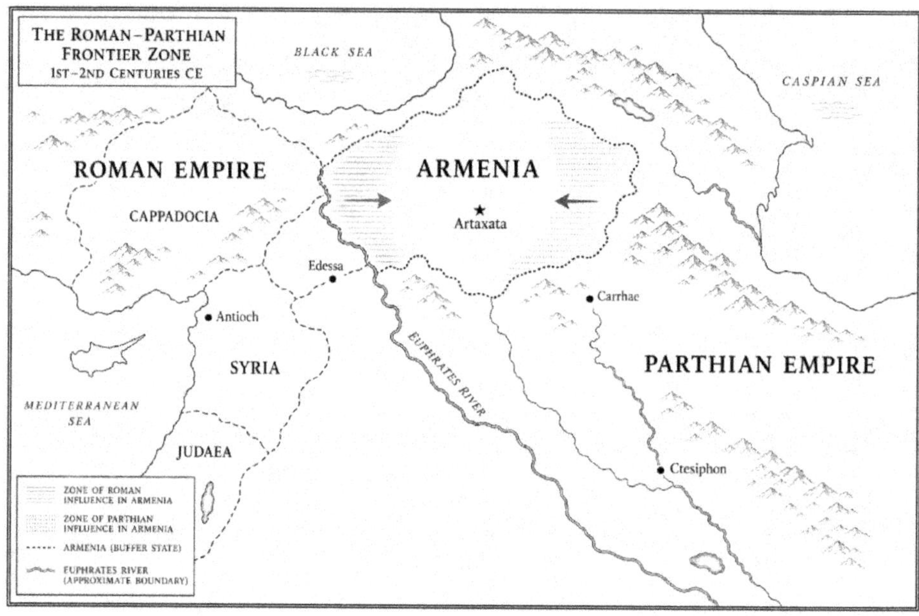

The Contested Frontier: Rome, Parthia, and Armenia, c. 1st–2nd Century CE

Between Rome and Parthia lay a mountainous kingdom neither could conquer and neither could ignore. For three centuries, Armenia was the fault line where the two empires repeatedly collided.

Armenia was a problem of geography before it was a problem of politics. Its highlands commanded the headwaters of the Tigris and Euphrates, the passes into Anatolia, and the roads leading south to Mesopotamia and north to the Caucasus. Whoever held Armenia held a dagger pointed at the other's heart, and both Rome and Ctesiphon understood this with uncomfortable clarity. The result was a peculiar dance that lasted from the late second century BCE to the fall of the Arsacid dynasty in 224 CE: invasions, coronations, marriages, betrayals, and the occasional treaty that pretended to settle what could not be settled. Armenia mattered not because it was rich, though it was not poor, but because it was the one place where two superpowers could not avoid touching each other. What follows traces that long entanglement from Tigranes the Great through the Treaty of Rhandeia and into the curious afterlife of a Parthian dynasty ruling an Armenian throne under Roman patronage - an arrangement so baroque it could only have been produced by exhaustion.

Tigranes the Great and the Roman Entanglement

Tigranes was born around 140 BCE into a world where Armenia was a second-rank kingdom and the Parthians were the new masters of Iran. As a young prince he was sent as a hostage to the Parthian court, a common enough fate for royal heirs in the ancient Near East, and there he waited while his father's kingdom shrank and his own prospects dimmed. When the throne came open in 95 BCE, it was the Parthians who put him on it, and they charged him a price: seventy valleys in the east, handed over as the cost of his freedom and his crown.

He paid. Then he spent the next four decades making the Parthians regret the bargain.

Tigranes was one of those figures who appear rarely in history - a ruler who grasps that the balance of power around him has shifted and acts on that knowledge faster than his neighbors can react. The Seleucid empire to his south was collapsing into the sectarian squabbles of its last, tired kings. The Parthians, for all their recent triumphs, were stretched thin in the east fighting nomadic incursions. Rome was busy with Mithridates of Pontus, who happened to be Tigranes's father-in-law. Into these gaps Tigranes marched.

He took back his seventy valleys. He pushed into Media and Mesopotamia, reducing Parthian vassals to his own. He swept south into Syria and, with the Seleucid dynasty in its death throes, was crowned king in Antioch itself. For a brief, startling decade, an Armenian king ruled from the Caucasus to the Mediterranean, titled himself King of Kings - a deliberate provocation aimed squarely at the Parthian monarch who had once held him hostage - and built a new capital, Tigranocerta, stuffed with Greek artisans and Hellenistic luxuries he had imported, sometimes at sword-point, from the cities he had conquered.

It was too good to last, and it did not. In 69 BCE the Roman general Lucullus crossed into Armenia and shattered Tigranes's field army outside his own new capital. Pompey finished the work three years later. Tigranes, now an old man, rode out to meet the Roman commander, dismounted, and laid his diadem at Pompey's feet. Pompey, in a gesture of theatrical magnanimity, picked it up and put it back on his head. Armenia would keep its king but lose its empire. Tigranes would pay six thousand talents and rule what remained as a Roman client.

The settlement mattered beyond the life of the man who accepted it. For the first time Rome had imposed its authority on the Armenian throne, and for the first time the Parthians had watched a western power dictate terms in a kingdom they considered their natural sphere. The precedent was poisonous. Every Armenian succession from that moment forward became a question that two empires felt entitled to answer, and the answers rarely matched.

Tigranes died in 55 BCE, aged around eighty-five, having outlived his rebellious son, his Pontic ally, and most of the Roman generals who had humbled him. He left behind a diminished kingdom and an unsolvable problem.

The Treaty of Rhandeia, 63 CE

For the next century the Armenian throne changed hands with dizzying frequency. Romans installed their candidates; Parthians installed theirs; local nobles quietly murdered whichever faction's man happened to be in residence. By the reign of Nero the pattern had hardened into crisis. In 54 CE the Parthian king Vologeses I placed his younger brother Tiridates on the Armenian throne, and Rome, unwilling to tolerate a full Arsacid takeover of its eastern flank, sent one of its most capable soldiers to dislodge him.

Gnaeus Domitius Corbulo was a Roman general of the old-fashioned kind - stern, methodical, and possessed of a fanatical concern for discipline. He spent two years whipping the eastern legions back into fighting shape, soldiers who had grown soft in Syrian garrisons and whom he reportedly forced to sleep in tents through an Armenian winter, before he moved. When he did, in 58 CE, he moved decisively. By 60 CE he had taken Artaxata and Tigranocerta and driven Tiridates out. Rome installed a puppet, Tigranes VI, a great-grandson of Herod raised in the capital, and seemed to have settled the matter.

It had not. Vologeses could not accept the humiliation of seeing his brother chased from the throne, and when Tigranes VI made the mistake of raiding Parthian client territory, Vologeses responded with a full campaign. Corbulo had by this time been reassigned to Syria, and command in Armenia passed to a less capable officer, Lucius Caesennius Paetus. In the autumn of 62 CE Paetus marched into Armenia with two legions, was surrounded by Parthian and Armenian forces at a place called Rhandeia on the upper Arsanias river, and after weeks of deteriorating conditions agreed to terms that amounted to surrender. His troops marched out under the yoke, abandoning their baggage, their wounded, and their dignity.

It was the worst Roman defeat in the east since Carrhae a century earlier, and it forced Nero's government to think seriously about what it actually wanted from Armenia. The answer, arrived at after another round of campaigning under the restored Corbulo, was a compromise so elegant that it held in one form or another for half a century.

The Treaty of Rhandeia, signed in 63 CE on the same plain where Paetus had surrendered, established a principle that historians sometimes call the Rhandeian formula. A Parthian prince of the Arsacid house would rule Armenia, but he would receive his crown from the hands of a Roman emperor. In practical terms, this meant that Tiridates - the man Rome had spent a decade trying to unseat - would keep his throne, but only after traveling to Rome and kneeling before Nero to receive his diadem.

The journey, when it came in 66 CE, was a piece of imperial theater unmatched in the first century. Tiridates crossed Asia Minor by land, refusing to board a ship because his Zoroastrian faith forbade him to pollute water. He brought with him three thousand Parthian cavalry and an entourage of magi. Nero met him at Puteoli with gladiatorial games, feasted him in Rome, crowned him in the Forum before vast crowds, and allowed him to rebuild the shattered city of Artaxata with Roman engineers and Roman money. Tiridates renamed it Neronia in his benefactor's honor.

Both sides claimed victory, which is often how successful treaties work. Rome retained the symbolic right to bestow the Armenian crown and could tell its citizens that the kingdom remained within the imperial orbit. Parthia retained the substance: an Arsacid on the throne, an Arsacid dynasty in Armenia, and a buffer kingdom that would not be turned into a Roman staging ground. For fifty years the arrangement largely worked. It did not end because it had failed. It ended because Trajan wanted it to.

A Parthian Dynasty on the Armenian Throne

The Arsacid line Tiridates founded in Armenia would, remarkably, outlast the Parthian Arsacids in Iran itself. When the Sasanians overthrew the last Parthian king in 224 CE, the Armenian branch of the family kept its throne for nearly two more centuries, ruling until 428 CE as the last custodians of a dynasty that had once governed an empire from the Euphrates to the Indus.

This was not an accident of geography. The Rhandeian settlement placed Armenia in a peculiar position, simultaneously attached to Parthia by blood and to Rome by ceremony. Every Armenian king from Tiridates onward inherited that doubleness. He spoke Parthian at home, corresponded in Greek with the Roman east, married into the Arsacid aristocracy of Mesopotamia, and accepted his crown - at least in principle - from a court on the Tiber. His army was organized on Iranian lines, with armored cataphracts drawn from the Armenian nobility, the nakharars, who held their lands on terms almost indistinguishable from the landholding system of the Parthian magnates.

The nakharars themselves were the second reason the Arsacid dynasty rooted so deeply in Armenia. Armenian society was structured around a handful of great noble houses, each controlling a province, a fortress network, and a private army. A king who tried to rule without their cooperation did not rule long. The Arsacid newcomers, products of a Parthian system built on exactly the same logic of aristocratic federation, understood the game instinctively. They co-opted rather than confronted, married into the leading houses, and in return received the kind of legitimacy no Roman-backed pretender had ever managed to secure. Tigranes VI, the Herodian puppet, had been a stranger speaking the wrong language. Tiridates was a kinsman speaking the right one.

Religion mattered too. Armenia in the first century CE was still a Zoroastrian kingdom in its elite culture, sharing with Parthia the fire-temples, the magi, and the Avestan liturgical tradition. Tiridates had refused to travel by sea out of ritual concern; his court in Armenia maintained the same observances. A Roman client, had one been permanently installed, would have had to govern through a religious establishment that viewed him as foreign. An Arsacid needed to do nothing but show up.

There was also the simple matter of administrative continuity. Parthian and Armenian nobles intermarried so regularly that by the second century it is sometimes impossible to sort them out in the surviving sources. A landowner might hold estates on both sides of the border, serve both kings, and count cousins in both courts. Rome's insistence on the Rhandeian ceremony imposed a formal boundary that social reality had already dissolved.

What resulted was a kingdom that looked, from Ctesiphon, like an extension of the Parthian world with a peculiar Roman accent. From Rome, it looked like a client state with an unusually independent foreign policy. Both descriptions were correct. The Armenian Arsacids had achieved what few dynasties in history have managed: they made ambiguity into a principle of government.

Proxy Wars and Diplomatic Marriages

The Rhandeian compromise did not end the quarrels over Armenia; it only changed their form. Rather than fight each other directly, Rome and Parthia learned to fight through Armenian factions, through succession disputes, and through the careful placement of brides.

When a king died in Artaxata, both empires scrambled to influence the choice of his successor. The Parthian candidate was almost always a kinsman of the reigning Arsacid king in Ctesiphon. The Roman candidate was often a rival Arsacid, perhaps a prince who had fled east-to-west during some dynastic quarrel and found refuge in Antioch or Rome. The elegance of the Roman position was that it could deploy members of the same family against each other, using the surplus princes of a dynasty famous for producing them.

Marriage was the other instrument. Armenian queens were drawn from the Parthian royal family as a matter of course, cementing the ties of blood and inheritance that made the Rhandeian settlement workable. When Rome wanted to shift the balance, it tried to insert brides from its own client kingdoms - Commagene, Cappadocia, the Herodian family - into the Armenian court. These matches rarely lasted, but they signaled intent, and they occasionally produced claimants whom Rome could promote when a throne fell vacant.

Trajan broke the pattern in 114 CE when he invaded Armenia, deposed its king, and annexed the kingdom outright as a Roman province. It was the most aggressive move Rome had made in the east since Crassus, and it was followed by an equally aggressive push into Mesopotamia, where Trajan briefly captured Ctesiphon itself. On paper it was the greatest Roman victory over Parthia ever recorded. In practice it collapsed almost immediately. The conquered territories rose in revolt, Trajan died in 117, and his successor Hadrian - always more concerned with consolidation than with glory - withdrew Roman forces from Armenia and Mesopotamia in 118, restoring the Arsacid arrangement that Trajan had torn up.

Hadrian's retreat vindicated the Rhandeian principle by showing what the alternative looked like. Direct rule was expensive, fragile, and rejected by the people it was imposed upon. An Arsacid on the throne, crowned by Rome and resident in Artaxata, cost nothing to maintain and provoked nobody. For the rest of the second century the formula largely held, with periodic spasms - Lucius Verus's war in the 160s, Septimius Severus's campaigns at the end of the century - that ended more or less where they began. The Armenian throne changed hands, but the principle of dual legitimacy survived.

What emerges from two centuries of this behavior is a portrait of ancient great-power competition that looks surprisingly modern. Neither empire wanted total war. Both wanted influence, prestige, and a buffer. The tools they developed - client rulers, succession interference, dynastic marriage, ceremonial coronation - would have been recognizable to any nineteenth-century diplomat working the Eastern Question.

Armenia as a Parthian Cultural Bridge

Armenia's political ambiguity produced a cultural richness that would have surprised observers in either capital. Sitting astride a trade corridor running from the Black Sea to northern Mesopotamia, the country carried goods, languages, and ideas through it in both directions.

The Armenian language itself, though classified by modern linguists as an independent branch of Indo-European, absorbed an enormous lexicon of Parthian loanwords during the Arsacid centuries. Terms for kingship, warfare, administration, religion, and aristocratic life came overwhelmingly from Parthian. When Armenian was finally committed to writing in the early fifth century, the alphabet invented by Mesrop Mashtots had to accommodate this deeply Iranian vocabulary. A modern Armenian reader encountering a fifth-century text meets Parthian on nearly every page.

Religious culture showed the same pattern. The Armenian gods of the pre-Christian period were recognizably Iranian in name and function: Aramazd corresponded to Ahura Mazda, Mihr to Mithra, Anahit to Anahita. Fire-temples dotted the highlands. The magi of Armenia, according to the Greek sources, were indistinguishable in practice from their Parthian counterparts. When Armenia converted to Christianity in the early fourth century - becoming, by tradition, the first kingdom in the world to do so as a matter of state - it did so against the cultural grain of an aristocracy that had been Zoroastrian for centuries, and the resulting synthesis carried Iranian vocabulary and concepts deep into Armenian Christian theology.

Art and architecture followed suit. The royal palaces of Artaxata and later Dvin were built on Parthian models, with audience halls and iwans - those vaulted, open-fronted chambers that would become the signature of later Iranian architecture. Armenian cavalry fought in the heavy Parthian style, armored from head to foot, and the lance techniques described in medieval

Armenian military texts preserve Arsacid tradition long after Arsacid rule had ended.

Armenia was also the conduit through which Hellenistic and Roman influences reached the Parthian world. Greek remained a language of administration and literature in the Armenian court well into the second century. Tigranes the Great had imported Greek artisans wholesale; their descendants stayed. Roman coins circulated alongside Parthian drachms. Architectural elements - columns, capitals, mosaic floors - crossed from west to east through Armenian workshops.

The kingdom was, in other words, exactly what its geography demanded it be: a place where the world's two halves met and borrowed from each other, mediated by a dynasty that belonged fully to neither.

Analysis

The Armenian Question reveals something important about how the Parthian empire actually worked. The Arsacids are often portrayed, particularly in Roman sources, as a purely military power whose statecraft began and ended with the cataphract charge. Armenia tells a different story. For three centuries the Parthian kings conducted a patient, sophisticated campaign of dynastic placement, cultural export, and diplomatic accommodation that secured their western flank at minimal cost. They lost battles along the way - Tigranes's humiliation, Corbulo's campaigns, Trajan's invasion - but they kept winning the longer game, because the man sitting on the Armenian throne was, more often than not, their cousin.

The Rhandeian formula was their greatest achievement in this arena. It gave Rome the ceremony Rome demanded and gave Parthia the substance Parthia wanted, and it held, with interruptions, until both empires were overthrown from within. Few diplomatic arrangements in the ancient world lasted longer or cost less blood to maintain.

Quick Summary

- Armenia's strategic position between Rome and Parthia made it the central flashpoint of their rivalry for three centuries.
- Tigranes the Great (r. 95-55 BCE) briefly built an Armenian empire before being crushed by Rome, establishing Roman claims over the Armenian throne.
- The Roman-Parthian War of 58-63 CE, fought over Armenia, ended with the Parthian-Armenian victory at Rhandeia in 62 CE.
- The Treaty of Rhandeia (63 CE) created a durable compromise: a Parthian Arsacid prince would rule Armenia but be crowned by the Roman emperor.
- Tiridates, the first king under this formula, traveled to Rome in 66 CE and was crowned by Nero in an elaborate ceremony.
- Trajan broke the treaty in 114 CE by annexing Armenia; Hadrian restored the Rhandeian arrangement in 118 CE.
- The Armenian Arsacid dynasty outlasted the Parthian parent line, ruling until 428 CE.
- Armenia became a cultural bridge, absorbing Parthian vocabulary, religion, and military technique while transmitting Hellenistic influences eastward.

Armenia's long balancing act matters because it shows, more clearly than almost any other episode in antiquity, that empires in contact need not be empires in permanent war. Rome and Parthia found, at Rhandeia, a way to share a border kingdom without destroying it or each other. The arrangement was imperfect, frequently violated, and occasionally forgotten, but it worked often enough and long enough to shape the cultural and political character of an entire region. When the Sasanians replaced the Arsacids in 224 CE, they inherited the Armenian problem along with everything else - and they would find, as their predecessors had, that the mountains between the empires could be neither conquered nor ignored.

Diplomacy over Armenia, like war with Rome and murder in the succession chamber, belonged to the world of kings. But empires are not only their crowned quarrels. Beneath the treaties and the coronations lay six or seven million people whose names appear in no chronicle: farmers, potters, widows, clerks, temple servants. The Arsacid system mattered to them less than their landlords and their harvests, and yet it was their quiet endurance that made the empire possible in the first place. To balance the view from the throne, we need the view from the courtyard.

Chapter 12:

Life Beyond the Court

Strip away the gold-plated thrones, the ambassadors in silk, the cavalry charges at Carrhae. What remains? A potter in a mudbrick courtyard in Babylonia. A widow in Susa arguing over a vineyard. A caravan clerk at Dura-Europos scribbling receipts in three alphabets. These are the Parthians the histories almost forgot.

The Arsacid court has dominated our story so far, and for good reason - the kings left us coins, palaces, and the anxious reports of Roman generals. But an empire of perhaps six or seven million souls was not a court. It was farmers flooding irrigation ditches in Khuzestan, weavers in Seleucia, shepherds on the Iranian plateau, dockworkers on the Euphrates. Their lives rarely made it into the chronicles, yet they are recoverable in fragments: parchments found in desert ruins, terracotta figurines in graves, marriage contracts scratched onto clay. What those fragments reveal is a society more plural, more mobile, and in some ways more generous to ordinary people than the Mediterranean world on the other side of the frontier.

Village Life in Mesopotamia and Iran

Most subjects of the Great King never saw him. They lived in villages of a few dozen families, in houses of mudbrick and thatch, within walking distance of fields their grandparents had worked. The rhythm of their year was set not by Arsacid politics but by water.

In lower Mesopotamia, the Tigris and Euphrates made agriculture possible and politics necessary. Canals had to be dredged, dikes repaired, water rights enforced. Under the Parthians, as under the Seleucids and Babylonians before them, this work fell on the village collectively, supervised by local headmen who answered, eventually, to a royal official. Wheat and barley were the staples; dates, sesame, and flax the cash crops. A single mature date palm could yield enough fruit to feed a family for months, and the Parthian south was a forest of them.

On the Iranian plateau the picture was different. Less water, more stone. Villages clung to the edges of mountain runoff or tapped the underground channels called qanats, patiently dug by specialists whose skills passed father to son. Farmers here grew hardier grains, grazed sheep and goats on the high pastures in summer, descended to walled settlements in winter. Horses - the famous Nisaean breed among them - were raised on royal and aristocratic estates in Media, the reservoir of Parthian cavalry power.

The social pyramid in both regions was steep but not simple. At its base stood peasants of varying status: some owned their land outright, some held it from a temple or a noble house in exchange for a share of the crop, some were bound more tightly still. Above them were village notables, local priests, and minor gentry. Higher up sat the *azatan*, the "free" warrior class who owed military service - the horse archers and cataphracts whose charges Rome learned to fear. And above the azatan, the seven great houses whose estates sprawled across entire provinces.

Yet the Arsacid state touched village life with a surprisingly light hand. Unlike the Roman system, which pressed its tax collectors and census takers into every crevice of provincial life, the Parthian administration largely delegated. Taxes were farmed out or collected through local intermediaries. Temples retained huge estates and considerable autonomy. Greek-style city councils continued to meet in Seleucia and Susa, minting their own coins and passing their own decrees long after those cities passed under Arsacid rule.

This light touch is sometimes read as weakness. It is better understood as a strategy. An empire stitched together from Greeks, Babylonians, Iranians,

Jews, Arabs, and nomadic Aramaeans could not be ruled the way Rome ruled Gaul. The Arsacids collected revenue, levied troops, and kept the roads open. In return, they mostly let village life go on as it had for centuries - the canals dredged in spring, the date harvest in autumn, the old gods worshipped at the old shrines.

For the peasant, this meant predictability, which in the ancient world was almost the same thing as good government.

Women, Marriage, and Property

A young woman in Susa around 100 BCE could sign her own marriage contract, own property in her own name, divorce her husband, and, if widowed, inherit his estate. None of these things was routinely possible for her counterpart in Rome or Athens. The contrast is one of the sharper surprises the Parthian world holds for modern readers.

The evidence comes from a scatter of documents - parchments from Dura-Europos, Greek inscriptions from Susa, cuneiform tablets from late Babylonia, and law codes compiled after the Parthians fell but still reflecting their era. The picture they produce is not of a feminist utopia. Parthian society was patriarchal and frequently brutal, and aristocratic women in particular were pieces on a marriage board, traded between the great houses to seal alliances. But within that world, women enjoyed legal capacities that stretched remarkably far.

Marriage contracts spell it out. A bride brought a dowry; the groom matched it with a counter-gift; both sums were tracked as her property, recoverable on divorce or widowhood. Several kinds of marriage existed, from the full "privileged" union that produced legitimate heirs to temporary or subsidiary arrangements with clearly defined rights. Polygamy was legal and, among the elite, common - kings and nobles maintained multiple wives and concubines - but each woman's status and her children's inheritance were laid down in writing.

Divorce could be initiated by either spouse in some arrangements, though men enjoyed the easier path. A woman whose husband proved impotent, cruel, or absent could petition to dissolve the union and recover her property. Widows often ended up managing estates, raising children, and conducting business in their own right. A Babylonian woman named Apollonia, known from a Seleucia tablet, appears selling a slave in her own name without a male guardian - a transaction that would have required her father or husband to stand behind her in most Greek cities.

Royal women wielded still greater power. The Arsacid queens - some Greek, some Iranian, some Armenian by origin - appear on coins, hold their own titles, and in several cases shape the succession. Musa, a slave-girl sent as a gift from Augustus to Phraates IV, rose to become queen, arranged her husband's poisoning, and ruled alongside her son Phraataces in the early first century CE. Her portrait, tiara and all, survives on coinage struck in her own name. She is an extreme case but not an isolated one; the Arsacids evidently accepted that a capable woman at court was an asset, not a scandal.

Outside the palace, the web of kinship still constrained most women tightly. A peasant wife in a Khuzestan village worked from dark to dark - grinding grain, tending children, spinning wool, hauling water. Girls married young, often to older men, and infant mortality was ferocious. Yet even here the legal substructure mattered. If her husband died, the land and the house did not automatically pass to a brother-in-law. She had standing. She had claims. She could go to court.

In the Mediterranean, the emancipation of women would be one of the slow revolutions of the modern age. In the Parthian east, something quieter and smaller but genuinely comparable had already happened, drawing on older Babylonian and Iranian traditions that never lost their grip.

Slavery and Dependent Labor

Parthian society was not free. It ran, as every ancient economy ran, on a graded spectrum of unfreedom, and at its bottom stood slaves.

They came from several sources. War supplied the greatest numbers. Every Parthian campaign against Rome, against Armenia, against rebellious vassals produced columns of captives driven east to be sold in the markets of Seleucia, Ctesiphon, and Ecbatana. Debt supplied others; a Babylonian farmer who could not pay his creditors might pledge a child, or himself, for a term of years. Children of slaves were slaves. Slaves could also be bought from traders moving goods along the steppe and desert routes - Sogdians, Arabs, Scythians - who dealt in human cargo alongside silk and spices.

What distinguished the Parthian system from the Roman was scale and intensity rather than kind. Rome's slave economy was industrial. Vast estates in Italy and Sicily worked by shackled gangs, mines swallowing tens of thousands, urban households staffed by dozens - this was a machine that consumed human beings at an appalling rate. The Parthian world had nothing comparable. Slaves were present in elite households, in workshops, in temples, in agriculture, but they worked alongside free peasants, tenant farmers, and other dependent laborers rather than replacing them.

Cuneiform and Greek documents from Seleucia and Susa record slave sales with the clinical precision of any bill of lading. A man named Nikanor buys a slave girl for a stated weight of silver; the seller guarantees her free of epilepsy and claims by other parties. Slaves could be manumitted, and manumission documents show former slaves acquiring property, marrying, and raising free children. Some temples specialized in ritual manumission, a practice borrowed from older Babylonian custom.

Between slavery and freedom lay a crowded zone of half-bound labor. Tenant farmers owed fixed shares to landlords. Temple dependents - called by various names in various regions - worked temple estates in exchange for rations and protection. Soldiers settled on military land held their plots in return for service and could not easily sell them. The azatan cavalry themselves were "free" precisely because others were not: their military freedom rested on peasants whose labor fed their horses.

Women in this empire enjoyed more law than their Mediterranean sisters; slaves endured a system less voracious than Rome's but no less cruel to the individual trapped inside it. The Arsacid world, like every premodern world, was built on backs.

Dura-Europos: A Frontier Town in Color

To walk through a Parthian town, walk through Dura-Europos. Thanks to a Roman siege that buried the place in sand in the 250s CE and a French-American excavation that unearthed it in the 1920s and 1930s, no other site from the eastern empire survives in such startling detail.

Dura stood on a bluff above the middle Euphrates, halfway between Mesopotamia and Syria. Founded around 300 BCE as a Seleucid garrison, it fell to the Parthians in 113 BCE and spent nearly three centuries as an Arsacid frontier town before Rome took it back in 165 CE. Those centuries under Parthian rule transformed it from a military outpost into a polyglot trading hub, and the excavators found the evidence written on its walls.

Literally written. Graffiti in Greek, Latin, Hebrew, Palmyrene, Hatran, Syriac, Middle Persian, and Parthian covered houses, barracks, and temples. Personal names recovered from the site run through every major ethnic group of the region - Semitic Abgars and Bargars, Iranian Arsaces and Tiridates, Greek Heliodorus and Apollodorus, an occasional Latin legionary name, Jewish patriarchs in the synagogue. The town was a shelf on which the whole Near East had left fingerprints.

Its temples tell the same story. A sanctuary of Bel and Yarhibol, the gods of Palmyra. A temple of Atargatis, the Syrian goddess. A shrine of the Gaddé, local fortune-deities. A temple of Artemis-Nanaia fusing Greek and Mesopotamian iconographies. A Mithraeum for the soldiers of the mystery cult. A synagogue whose walls were painted with extraordinary biblical scenes - Moses at the burning bush, the Exodus, Esther before Ahasuerus - executed in the frontal, wide-eyed style that scholars now call Parthian art. And, most famously, a Christian house-church with some of the earliest surviving Christian wall paintings anywhere on earth, including a baptistery where Christ walks on water and the women approach the empty tomb.

All of this in a town of perhaps five or six thousand people.

Domestic life at Dura was equally layered. Houses were built around courtyards in the old Mesopotamian pattern, but furnished with Greek-style dining couches for banquets. Women dressed in belted tunics and veils; men wore the long trousers and tunics that the Greeks had once mocked as barbaric and now copied. Caravan merchants from Palmyra set up way-stations and married local women. Parthian garrison commanders lived in a small citadel on the bluff. A Roman mural of Julius Terentius, tribune of the 20th Palmyrene cohort, sacrificing before three gods, was painted over an earlier Parthian-style mural in the same temple - the town's gods accumulated worshippers the way its walls accumulated graffiti.

Dura is not typical. Frontier cities never are. But it is precious because it preserves, in unusual fullness, the texture of a world that was pluralist not by ideology but by habit. Nobody at Dura had decided to build a multicultural society. They simply lived in one, because the caravan routes required it and the Arsacid government permitted it.

Clothing, Food, and the Parthian Banquet

The Parthians gave the world trousers. Or at least they pressed the fashion so hard on their Mediterranean neighbors that the Greeks and Romans, who had scorned them, eventually gave in.

Parthian dress, visible on reliefs, coins, and the painted walls of Dura, was the costume of a horse people made elegant. Men wore a long belted tunic, often elaborately embroidered, over baggy trousers gathered at the ankle and tucked into soft boots. A short cloak, pinned at the shoulder, topped the outfit. Hair was worn long, curled and bound with a diadem among the nobility. Women wore ankle-length robes, belted high, with long sleeves and a veil draped from the crown of the head. Jewelry was abundant - earrings, torcs, bracelets, rings - and Parthian textiles, patterned in medallions and plant motifs, became luxury exports to Rome.

Food was regional. In Mesopotamia: barley bread, date syrup, fish from the rivers, beer, lamb stewed with onions and pulses. In Iran: wheat bread, yogurt, goat and mutton, pomegranates, nuts, the sour tang of dried fruits in savory dishes. Wine traveled everywhere the Greeks had settled and well beyond. The fat-tailed sheep of the steppe provided both meat and cooking fat. Spices moved west along the caravan routes - long pepper and cinnamon from India, saffron from Media - and worked their way into the pots of those who could afford them.

The aristocratic banquet was the set piece. Parthian reliefs show nobles reclining on couches in a style inherited from Greek practice but adapted to Iranian taste: guests stretched out singly or in pairs, servants pouring from long-necked jugs, musicians at the edges. Hunting preceded the meal. A good host took his guests out after boar or gazelle in the royal paradises - walled game reserves stocked for the purpose - and the kill was roasted that evening.

The drinking was serious. Greek and Roman visitors, no strangers to wine themselves, reported on Parthian capacity with grudging admiration. Conversation ranged over poetry, politics, and genealogy; the Parthian elite was immensely proud of its lineages. Music was central. The *gosan*, the bardic poet-singer, held a respected place at noble feasts, performing heroic tales and love laments that would later feed into the Persian epic tradition.

These banquets were not mere indulgence. They were the social glue of an aristocratic federation. Oaths were sworn, alliances struck, marriages arranged around the low tables. A king who could not host a good feast was in political trouble.

Patterns

Step back from the detail, and a pattern emerges. The Parthian world was less centralized than Rome, less uniform than Han China, less intrusive in the daily lives of its subjects than either. It was a confederation of regions, languages, and faiths held together by a royal house, a cavalry class, and a network of roads and rivers. Below the level of the court, an enormous amount of life simply continued as it had for centuries, with local elites, local gods, and local law codes going about their business.

This has sometimes been read as the reason the Parthians "failed" - why they produced no Virgil, no monumental code, no unifying administrative language. But it is also why they lasted nearly five centuries in a region that had chewed up every previous empire within two hundred years. Light government, tolerated difference, and a flexible elite kept the system viable across terrain no bureaucracy of the period could have micromanaged. The peasant kept her land; the merchant at Dura kept his gods; the widow in Susa kept her vineyard. In exchange, they kept the Arsacids.

It is not a romantic story. Slavery ground on. Warfare was constant. Famine and plague struck without warning. But measured against its neighbors, Parthian society offered its ordinary people something approaching a workable bargain - and that, in the ancient world, was rarer than gold.

Quick Summary

- Most Parthian subjects lived in villages governed by local custom, with the imperial state taking a notably light hand compared to Rome.
- Agriculture depended on canal irrigation in Mesopotamia and qanat-fed fields on the Iranian plateau; date palms and grain were the staples.
- Women enjoyed significant legal rights - to own property, sign contracts, divorce, and inherit - far exceeding those of their Greek and Roman contemporaries.
- Slavery existed but on a smaller and less industrial scale than in Rome, surrounded by a wide spectrum of tenant and dependent labor.
- Dura-Europos, taken by the Parthians in 113 BCE, preserves the fullest surviving picture of a Parthian provincial town - polyglot, multireligious, and deeply cosmopolitan.
- Parthian dress (tunic, trousers, cloak) and aristocratic banquets (reclining feasts with music and hunting) became cultural exports felt as far as Rome.
- The empire's tolerance of local difference was both its political strategy and its durability.

The Arsacids built their superpower not by flattening the peoples under them but by leaving most of their lives alone. When the dynasty finally fell in 224 CE, the villages, the marriage contracts, the banquets, the painted temples at Dura would all continue under new masters. The court changed. The world beneath it, in large part, did not - and that silent continuity is the Parthians' most underestimated legacy.

The villages went on. The marriage contracts were drawn up, the vineyards argued over, the banquets held. But along the Euphrates the quiet continuity of daily life was periodically broken by something louder - a Roman emperor with seven legions, convinced that this time the Parthian problem would be solved. After Carrhae, Rome kept coming back, and each return tested both the resilience of Arsacid society and the patience of the kings who had to defend it. The long wars with Rome, from Mark Antony to Septimius Severus, form their own bleak chapter.

Chapter 13:

Trajan, Lucius Verus, and the Long Roman Wars

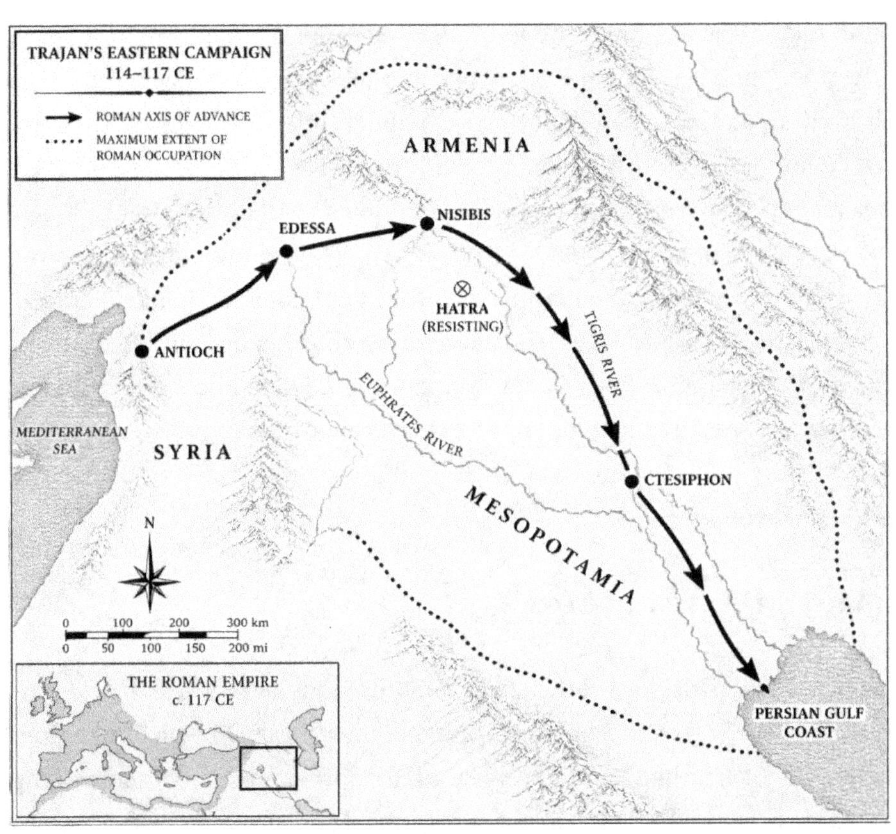

Trajan's Eastern Campaign, 114–117 CE

After Carrhae, Rome kept coming back. Emperor after emperor tried to solve the Parthian problem by force, and each campaign revealed both the limits of Roman power and the extraordinary resilience of the Arsacid state.

For nearly three centuries, the Euphrates was the line that Rome could cross but could not truly hold. Mark Antony learned it in the mountains of Media. Trajan learned it on the marshes of southern Mesopotamia. Lucius Verus appeared to solve it, then carried home a catastrophe worse than any battlefield defeat. Septimius Severus stormed into Ctesiphon and rode back with glory that tasted remarkably like his predecessors'. Each campaign followed a pattern so consistent it reads almost like ritual: invasion, early victory, the sack of a Parthian city, the proud assumption of eastern titles, then retreat. The Parthians absorbed the blows, withdrew into their vast interior, harassed supply columns, and waited. They did not need to win the war. They only needed to outlast Rome's logistics, Rome's climate tolerance, and the patience of the legionaries sweltering four hundred miles from the nearest friendly coast. Four Roman emperors tried, and one exiled triumvir tried first, to break the empire on the eastern side of the river. None of them succeeded. Understanding why is essential to understanding what the Parthians really were.

Antony's Disaster in Media

Mark Antony had every advantage Crassus had lacked. He had Julius Caesar's old officers and a hundred thousand men, a careful plan drawn from the lessons of Carrhae, and a promise of support from the Armenian king Artavasdes. In 36 BCE he marched for the Median capital of Phraaspa determined to erase the humiliation of 53 BCE and hand Rome the east that Caesar had been assassinated before he could take.

The plan was elegant on paper. Antony would leave his siege train with a rear guard under Oppius Statianus while the main army pressed ahead into Media Atropatene. Phraaspa, once taken, would become the anchor of a new

Roman province. The Parthian king Phraates IV, still young and still insecure on a throne he had taken by killing his father, would either sue for peace or be destroyed.

Instead, the mountains and the horsemen did their work. The column moved too fast. Statianus fell behind. A Parthian cavalry force caught the siege train in open country, annihilated the two legions guarding it, killed Statianus, and burned the rams and towers Antony had spent months building. Artavasdes of Armenia, watching from a careful distance, took his cavalry and went home.

Antony reached Phraaspa with a hungry army and no way to breach its walls. He tried anyway. For weeks his men raised earthworks under a sky full of arrows, while the defenders sortied at night to tear them down. Autumn came early in the Median highlands. Food ran short. The Parthians refused pitched battle and simply watched.

The retreat that followed, in October and November of 36 BCE, was one of the worst marches in Roman military history. Plutarch, drawing on the memoirs of a companion who had been there - a man named Dellius - describes twenty-seven days of running fight across 300 miles of broken country. Parthian archers shadowed the column from every ridge. Horse-archers struck whenever the legions fell out of testudo formation. Thirst drove men to drink from poisoned streams. Frostbite took fingers and feet. When the survivors finally crossed into Armenia, Antony had lost perhaps 20,000 legionaries and 4,000 cavalry, roughly a third of the force that had set out.

He blamed Artavasdes, and later had him executed in chains. But the truth was simpler. The Median campaign failed for the same reason every Roman campaign east of the Euphrates would struggle for the next two and a half centuries: the Parthians had mastered the art of not being where the Romans wanted them to be, and of being everywhere the Romans did not. Antony never tried again. Within six years he was dead in Alexandria, and the eastern problem passed to Augustus, who was wise enough to negotiate rather than invade.

Trajan's Mesopotamian Campaign, 114-117 CE

A hundred and fifty years later, Rome tried the largest eastern offensive in its history. Trajan was sixty-one years old in 114 CE, a veteran of the Dacian Wars, an emperor whose popularity at home rested on a record of unbroken military success. He had conquered Dacia and added its gold mines to the imperial treasury. He meant to do the same for Mesopotamia, and perhaps for more.

The immediate pretext was Armenian. The Parthian king Osroes I had deposed a Roman client and installed his own nephew on the Armenian throne without consulting Rome. Under the settlement Augustus and Nero had both upheld, Armenia was supposed to be a shared client - proposed by Parthia, confirmed by Rome. Osroes had broken the rule. Trajan seized on it.

What followed looked at first like textbook Roman conquest. In 114 Trajan marched through Armenia, deposed the Arsacid claimant, and annexed the whole kingdom as a Roman province. In 115 he turned south into northern Mesopotamia, taking Nisibis and Edessa. The Parthian empire was in the middle of a dynastic civil war between Osroes and a rival claimant, Vologases III, and could mount nothing coordinated against him. In 116 Trajan did what no Roman commander had ever done before. He took Ctesiphon, the Parthian capital, and captured the royal throne along with a daughter of Osroes. He sailed down the Tigris to the Persian Gulf and, according to Cassius Dio, watched a merchant ship set out for India and wished he were younger.

Then everything came apart. The problem with taking Parthian cities was that taking them did not end the war. Trajan had occupied enormous stretches of territory with garrisons that were, by Roman standards, thin. As soon as he reached the Gulf, the Mesopotamian cities behind him rose in coordinated revolt. Seleucia, Nisibis, Edessa, Hatra - every major center flared into rebellion. A Parthian prince named Sanatruces raised an army and began reclaiming the north. Roman commanders had to be peeled off to fight simultaneous fires.

Trajan himself marched on Hatra, the fortress-city in the Syrian desert that guarded the caravan routes. Hatra's walls, its wells, and its ferocious summer sun defeated him. The Roman camp broiled. Men and horses collapsed from heat and thirst. Arab cavalry harassed the foraging parties. After weeks of fruitless assault, the emperor who had taken Ctesiphon lifted the siege and retreated.

He was already ill. In the summer of 117, heading back toward Rome to organize a new offensive, Trajan suffered what was probably a stroke. He died at Selinus in Cilicia in August. His successor, Hadrian, drew a conclusion that would shape Roman policy for a century. The Mesopotamian provinces were indefensible. Within months, Hadrian had abandoned them, pulled the frontier back to the Euphrates, and restored Armenia to client status.

Trajan's campaign remains one of the strangest episodes in Roman military history. By every immediate measure it was a triumph: he had taken the enemy capital, reached the ocean, and seen his legions farther east than any Roman army before or after. By every strategic measure it was a failure. The moment he turned his back, the territory he had conquered dissolved. The Parthian state, fractured and leaderless, still proved impossible to absorb. A lesson was available for anyone who wanted to read it. Hadrian read it. His successors, eventually, chose not to.

Lucius Verus and the Plague That Came Home

When Antoninus Pius died peacefully in 161 CE, the Parthian king Vologases IV tested the new regime almost immediately. He invaded

Armenia, deposed the Roman client king Sohaemus, and installed an Arsacid of his own. A Roman governor of Cappadocia, Severianus, rushed north with a legion to restore the situation. At Elegeia, the legion was surrounded and destroyed. Severianus killed himself. Parthian cavalry then poured into Syria.

Marcus Aurelius and his adopted brother Lucius Verus had been emperors for barely a year. They divided the work. Marcus remained in Rome. Verus, thirty years old, went east as the face of Roman response. The real planning was done by a cadre of experienced generals - Avidius Cassius, Statius Priscus, Martius Verus - who understood that the eastern war would be won or lost on logistics and discipline rather than imperial charisma.

It took them two years to rebuild. Legions were transferred from the Danube. Supply dumps were established in Antioch. Discipline, which had gone slack under decades of peace, was restored by ferocious commanders. Then in 163 Statius Priscus struck north into Armenia and retook Artaxata. A new Roman client was installed in a new capital, pointedly renamed Kainepolis, the New City.

The main offensive came in 164 and 165. Avidius Cassius drove down the Euphrates, broke a Parthian army at Dura-Europos, and pushed on toward the heart of Mesopotamia. Edessa fell. Nisibis fell. In 165 Cassius took Seleucia, the great Greek city on the Tigris, and then crossed to Ctesiphon itself. The royal palace was burned. Vologases fled. For the second time in fifty years, a Roman army stood in the Parthian capital.

Verus, operating mostly from Antioch and Ephesus, collected the titles: *Armeniacus, Parthicus Maximus, Medicus*. Coins were struck. Monuments were planned. By Roman standards the war was a triumphant success, a proper answer to Elegeia, and a vindication of the new regime.

And then the soldiers came home, and they brought something with them.

The ancient sources are vague about its origin. A story circulated that Roman troops in Seleucia had broken into a sealed temple of Apollo and released a pestilence imprisoned there. The story is obviously a morality tale about sacrilege, but it preserves something real: contemporaries believed the disease had come from the east with the returning army. Modern historians have generally identified it as smallpox, though measles and other candidates have been proposed. Its name in the sources is the Antonine Plague.

It spread along the same roads the legions marched. By 166 it was in Syria. By 167 it was in Rome. Galen, who saw it firsthand, described pustules, black diarrhea, fever, and death within days. Cassius Dio, writing later, reported 2,000 deaths per day in Rome at the peak. Modern estimates of total mortality across the empire range from 10 to 25 percent of the population over fifteen years - somewhere between seven and fifteen million people.

Lucius Verus himself died in 169, probably of the plague, on a journey north with Marcus Aurelius to fight the Marcomanni on the Danube. He was thirty-nine. His military reputation, enhanced by his generals, survived him. The plague did not. It hollowed out the legions at the exact moment when the northern frontier was collapsing, forced Marcus Aurelius to recruit slaves and gladiators into the army, and shadowed Roman demographics for a generation. The greatest victory against Parthia in Roman history turned out to be the most expensive.

Septimius Severus Sacks Ctesiphon

A generation later, the pattern repeated. Septimius Severus, the North African general who had won the civil wars of 193-197 CE, needed a foreign triumph to legitimize a reign that had begun in Roman blood. Parthia provided it. The Parthian king Vologases V had supported Severus's rival Pescennius Niger during the civil war and had used the Roman distraction to raid the frontier. The pretext for retaliation was ready-made.

Severus's campaign of 197-198 CE followed the Trajanic script with almost uncanny precision. He marched down the Euphrates in boats built at Zeugma. He bypassed the desert fortresses. He took Seleucia without resistance - the city had been declining since the last sack - and in early 198 he stormed Ctesiphon. The sack was savage. Cassius Dio, our main source, reports that the Romans killed the male population, enslaved 100,000 women and children, and carried off an enormous treasure. Severus proclaimed himself *Parthicus Maximus* and dated the founding of a new province, Mesopotamia, from the victory.

Then he turned to Hatra, and the script snapped back to Trajan's version. Twice, in 198 and 199, Severus besieged the desert fortress. Twice he failed. His siege engines were burned by Hatrene incendiaries - the ancient sources describe a naphtha weapon that clung and burned through armor. His European troops mutinied in the heat. His Praetorian Guard refused an assault. He lifted the siege and went home, claiming the larger victory and not mentioning the smaller defeat.

What Severus did differently was consolidation. He kept Nisibis and made it the capital of the new province of Mesopotamia, permanently garrisoned by two new legions, I and III Parthica. He fortified the Khabur line. The frontier moved east - not by much, but for the first time Rome held a strip of territory beyond the Euphrates that it would continue to hold, with interruptions, until the seventh century.

The strategic logic of the campaign was the same as all the others, however. Rome could reach Ctesiphon. Rome could burn Ctesiphon. Rome could not keep Ctesiphon. The Parthian state absorbed the blow, as it had absorbed Trajan's and Verus's, and the Arsacid dynasty stumbled on for another quarter century - weakened, increasingly unable to project power, but still in place.

That weakening would matter. Within twenty-five years of Severus's sack, the Arsacid house would fall - not to Rome, but to a rebellion from within its own empire, led by a Persian nobleman named Ardashir from the province of Fars. The Romans had not destroyed Parthia. They had exhausted it.

Why Rome Could Not Hold What It Took

Five campaigns. Three sacks of Ctesiphon. Two annexations of Mesopotamia, both reversed. One catastrophic retreat from Media. And one plague that killed more Romans than any Parthian army ever had. What should we make of the pattern?

Begin with logistics. A Roman army operating east of the Euphrates was at the end of a supply tether four hundred miles long, running through country with limited fodder and hostile summers. The legions could bring food for a campaigning season. They could not bring food for a province. The great Mesopotamian cities - Seleucia, Ctesiphon, Babylon - depended on irrigation networks that required local knowledge and local labor. Roman garrisons dropped into this system were parasites. They could take cities. They could not run them.

Add politics. The Parthian empire was not a centralized state in the Roman sense. It was a confederation of client kings, noble houses, and Greek cities bound to the Arsacid dynasty by treaty and tradition. When Rome took Ctesiphon, it took a capital but not a government. The Arsacids simply moved east, regrouped among the Parthian nobility of the highlands, and waited. Their authority did not depend on holding one city. Rome's occupation did.

Add the geography of cavalry. Every Roman campaign east of the Euphrates had to contend with the fact that Parthian horse-archers could move faster than Roman legions and attack supply lines with near impunity. The *cataphract* - the armored heavy lancer - handled anything that tried to break out of formation. The combination meant that Roman columns could reach their objectives but could not dominate the space between objectives. That space - the open ground of northern Mesopotamia and the Iranian plateau - was Parthian by default.

Finally, add disease. The Antonine Plague was the most dramatic example, but every eastern campaign suffered from what the Romans called the summer fevers. Malaria, dysentery, heat exhaustion, and the unnamed viruses of a densely populated commercial zone killed more legionaries than arrows did. Every emperor who marched east paid a tax in men that never appeared in the triumph inscriptions.

The Parthians, for their part, learned to fight a war of depth. They gave up capitals and kept kingdoms. They traded Ctesiphon for time, because time was the thing Rome could not manufacture. It was not a glamorous strategy. It did not produce the set-piece victories that ancient historians liked to write about. But it worked for three hundred years.

Key Figures & Events

Mark Antony's Median campaign of 36 BCE lost roughly 24,000 men and ended any Roman hope of conquering Media. Trajan's campaign of 114-117 CE reached the Persian Gulf but collapsed on contact with rebellion and disease; Hadrian abandoned the conquests within a year. Lucius Verus and his generals - Avidius Cassius, Statius Priscus, Martius Verus - sacked Ctesiphon in 165 CE and imported the Antonine Plague, which killed perhaps ten percent of the Roman population. Septimius Severus sacked Ctesiphon again in 198 CE but failed twice at Hatra and settled for annexing the province of Mesopotamia with Nisibis as its anchor. Vologases IV and Vologases V, the Parthian kings facing Verus and Severus, lost capitals but kept their thrones.

Analysis

The long Roman wars against Parthia are often described as a stalemate. That is not quite right. Rome won nearly every campaign it fought. It took the Parthian capital three times. It added Armenian territory and, under Severus, a permanent foothold in upper Mesopotamia. Judged by battles, Rome was dominant.

Judged by consequences, the picture inverts. The Arsacid dynasty outlasted eight Roman emperors who campaigned against it. The Parthian state, though weakened, was not conquered - and when it finally fell, in 224 CE, it fell to a Persian rebel from within, not to a Roman invader from without. Meanwhile, the wars cost Rome enormous treasure, tens of thousands of soldiers, and, in the case of Verus's campaign, a plague that may have been the single greatest demographic catastrophe of the ancient Mediterranean.

Parthia's genius was not military innovation, though its cavalry was formidable. It was strategic patience married to decentralized political structure. A state that does not depend on a single capital cannot be decapitated. A society organized around nobles and client kings can lose its royal city and still function. Rome, the most centralized empire the ancient world had ever seen, kept fighting Parthia as if Parthia worked the same way. It did not. That misunderstanding, repeated across three centuries, is what the long wars were really about.

Quick Summary

- Mark Antony invaded Media in 36 BCE with 100,000 men and lost roughly a third of them in a catastrophic retreat; he never tried again.
- Trajan in 114-117 CE conducted the largest eastern offensive in Roman history, taking Armenia, Mesopotamia, and Ctesiphon, before revolt and death forced withdrawal.

- Hadrian abandoned Trajan's conquests almost immediately, concluding that Mesopotamia could not be held.
- Lucius Verus's generals, led by Avidius Cassius, sacked Ctesiphon in 165 CE in apparent triumph.
- The returning army brought the Antonine Plague, which killed between 10 and 25 percent of the Roman population over fifteen years.
- Septimius Severus sacked Ctesiphon again in 198 CE and annexed the province of Mesopotamia, but failed twice to take Hatra.
- Every Roman campaign reached its objective and none could hold the ground taken, owing to logistics, geography, cavalry warfare, and disease.
- The Parthian state survived three hundred years of Roman pressure and fell, in the end, to an internal Persian revolt in 224 CE.

Rome remembered these wars as triumphs. The triumphal arches still stand in fragments. The coins still survive, with their proud legends of *Parthicus Maximus* and *Armeniacus*. But behind the monuments lies a stranger story, in which an empire that could not be matched on any battlefield kept marching to the Tigris and kept marching home with less than it had set out with. The Parthians never wrote that story down. They did not need to. They simply kept being there, kingdom after kingdom, generation after generation, until a man from Fars decided the Arsacids had ruled long enough. That is the subject of the next chapter.

Rome could march to Ctesiphon and still march home with less than it came for, because the Arsacids had something Rome rarely appreciated: the luxury of a second front that demanded their real attention. While emperors boasted of Parthicus Maximus on their coins, Arsacid kings were often looking the other way, toward the Hindu Kush and the steppe passes, where kingdoms and confederations rose and fell faster than any Roman could track. The eastern frontier was where the empire was tested most severely, and it deserves to be seen on its own terms.

Chapter 14:

The Eastern Frontier

Look at a map of the ancient world and your eye drifts, almost automatically, toward the Euphrates. That is where Rome and Parthia met, where legions drowned and emperors schemed. But turn the map around. Face east, toward the Hindu Kush and the Pamirs, and you see the frontier that gave Arsacid kings more sleepless nights than any Roman ever did.

For most of their five-century reign, the Parthians were a two-front empire. To the west, the Romans were a known quantity: disciplined, predictable, held in check by geography and grain supplies. To the east, the world was stranger and less forgiving. Bactria and the satrapies beyond the Iranian plateau were buffeted by wave after wave of horsemen from the steppe - Sakas, Yuezhi, Kushans - whose movements were driven by forces the Arsacids could neither predict nor control. Losing a legion was a humiliation. Losing Bactria was a structural defeat that reshaped the empire. What follows traces the Parthians eastward, into the wars, the trade treaties, and the cultural exchanges that historians, drunk on Roman sources, have too often ignored. The story of Parthia cannot be told without the Kushans, the Indo-Parthians of the Punjab, and the Buddhist monks who remembered Iranian names long after the Arsacids were dust.

The Loss of Bactria and the Rise of the Kushans

Bactria, the fertile country straddling the Oxus river in what is now northern Afghanistan and southern Uzbekistan, was the eastern heart of the Hellenistic world. Alexander's veterans had settled there. Greek kings had minted some of the finest coins of antiquity in its cities. For the early

Arsacids, Bactria was the prize that hovered always at the edge of ambition - a rich, urbanized province that, if taken, would bind the Iranian plateau together as it had been under the Achaemenids.

Mithridates I, the architect of Parthian greatness between 171 and 138 BCE, understood this better than anyone. His armies pushed east as well as west, pressing into Margiana and the fringes of Bactria, winning victories that seemed to herald full absorption. But Mithridates was fighting on two fronts at once, and the eastern campaign was never finished. The Greek kingdom of Bactria, already fragmenting into rival principalities, collapsed - but not into Parthian hands.

What arrived instead was the steppe. In the late second century BCE, a confederation the Chinese chronicles called the Yuezhi came tumbling out of Central Asia, displaced by the Xiongnu and looking for land. They rolled over the last Greek kings of Bactria like a flood over a sandcastle. Behind them came Saka groups, also moving west and south. For a generation, the region was a churn of competing warbands, and the Parthians found their eastern flank not occupied by a conquerable Greek satrapy but by something far worse: a reservoir of horse archers as skilled as their own.

The Arsacids paid in blood. Two Parthian kings, Phraates II and Artabanus I, died in battle against these eastern nomads in the 120s BCE - a catastrophic decade that nearly destroyed the young empire. Phraates fell fighting Saka auxiliaries he himself had hired; Artabanus was killed in a campaign in the northeast. The western frontier went unguarded. Mithridates II, who eventually stabilized the situation, did so by accepting what his predecessors could not: the east would have to be managed, bribed, and partitioned, not conquered.

Out of the Yuezhi chaos, one clan eventually rose to dominance. They called themselves the Kushans. By the first century CE they had welded the scattered principalities of Bactria into a single kingdom, and under their greatest ruler, Kanishka - who reigned in the early second century CE, traditionally dated around 127 to 150 - they built an empire that stretched from the Aral Sea to the Ganges valley.

The Kushans were not simply another nomadic horde. They minted gold coins in astonishing quantities, patronized Buddhism and Zoroastrianism and Greek gods indifferently, and ran the overland trade that connected China to the Mediterranean. For the Parthians, this was a mixed inheritance. The Kushans were too strong to defeat but, crucially, they pointed south and east rather than west. Bactria was lost forever - no Arsacid army ever ruled in Balkh again - but the frontier settled into a wary, often profitable, coexistence. It was one of the quieter tragedies of Parthian history: the richest province of the east, slipped from their grasp in the chaos of the second century BCE, became instead the base of a rival superpower.

The Indo-Parthian Kingdom of Gondophares

If Bactria was lost, something stranger happened further south. In the first century CE, a dynasty calling itself Parthian - or at least claiming Arsacid legitimacy - emerged not in Iran but in what is now Pakistan and southern Afghanistan. Its greatest king, Gondophares, ruled from around 19 to 46 CE over a patchwork realm stitched together from the ruins of the Indo-Greek and Saka kingdoms of the Indus basin.

Gondophares is a figure who sits at the seam between history and legend. His coins survive in the thousands, bilingual in Greek and Kharoshthi script, bearing his bearded profile and proud titles: *Great King of Kings*, the old Achaemenid formula given new life in the Punjab. He controlled the Kabul valley, Gandhara, Sindh, and stretches of the Indus plain. His capital was probably at Taxila, the ancient university city whose ruins still crowd a dusty valley north of Islamabad.

Who exactly these Indo-Parthians were is a puzzle historians have not fully solved. Their rulers bore Iranian names; their court titles echoed those of Ctesiphon; their cavalry fought in Parthian style. Yet they were not, so far as we can tell, appointees of the Arsacid king. Rather, they seem to have been a cadet branch, or perhaps a noble house of Parthian origin that had carved out its own kingdom on the imperial fringe, taking advantage of the fragmentation of Saka power. They were Parthian in the way that Norman Sicily was Norman - a transplanted warrior aristocracy ruling over a different cultural substrate.

Gondophares is remembered for more than his coins. In the apocryphal *Acts of Thomas*, a Syriac Christian text probably composed in the third century, the apostle Thomas is said to have traveled to the court of a king named Gudnaphar in India, converting him to Christianity. For centuries this was dismissed as pure legend. Then, in the nineteenth century, coins bearing the name Gondophares were found in the Punjab, and scholars realized that the legend had attached itself to a real ruler, at the right time, in the right place. Whether Thomas actually reached Taxila is anyone's guess. That Indian Christians believed he did, and named a Parthian king as his royal patron, tells us something about how far east the reach of Iranian political culture extended.

The Indo-Parthian kingdom did not last. Within a generation of Gondophares's death, the Kushans pushed south from Bactria and absorbed most of his territories. By the reign of Kanishka, the Indus valley was firmly Kushan. But the Indo-Parthian century left permanent marks. Gandharan sculpture - the extraordinary fusion of Greek, Indian, and Iranian styles that produced the first figural images of the Buddha - took shape under Indo-Parthian and early Kushan patronage. The drapery of a Gandharan bodhisattva owes as much to a Parthian nobleman's robes as to any Hellenistic model.

For the Arsacids in distant Ctesiphon, the Indo-Parthian kingdom was a curious cousin rather than a province. There is no evidence that Gondophares paid tribute or took orders from the Great King. What the Arsacids gained was something more diffuse: a reminder that Parthian political forms - the kingship, the cavalry aristocracy, the trilingual coinage - could travel, root themselves in foreign soil, and flourish independently of the imperial center. The Parthian world, it turned out, was wider than the Parthian state.

Saka Pressure on the Eastern Marches

Between the Kushans in Bactria and the Indo-Parthians in the Punjab lay a third force that harried the Arsacids throughout their history: the Sakas. The Greeks called them Scythians, which was really a catch-all term for Iranian-speaking nomads of the steppe. By the late second century BCE, Saka bands, pushed south by the same Yuezhi migrations that had ended Greek Bactria, spilled into the eastern Parthian provinces.

The region that bears their name to this day is Sistan - originally Sakastan, *the land of the Sakas*. This rugged borderland of eastern Iran and southern Afghanistan absorbed so many Saka settlers that it effectively became their country, even while remaining nominally under Arsacid suzerainty. The Parthian response to the Saka problem was the response of most empires to nomadic pressure: a mixture of war, recruitment, and managed settlement.

Phraates II tried war first. He hired Saka mercenaries against the Seleucids, then quarreled with them over pay, and ended up dead in 128 BCE when his own hired horsemen defected and joined the Saka invasion he had meant to repel. Artabanus I, his successor, died a few years later on the same frontier. These were not minor skirmishes. An empire that lost two kings in a decade to a single enemy was an empire in existential crisis.

Mithridates II, who reigned from around 124 to 88 BCE, changed the strategy. Rather than trying to drive the Sakas out, he incorporated them. Saka chieftains were given land, titles, and a role in the imperial system. Sakastan was allowed to remain Saka in culture and population, with its own dynasts who acknowledged the Great King. It was an elegant solution, and one the Romans, with their tidier conception of sovereignty, rarely managed.

A Parthian satrapy did not have to be ethnically Parthian; it had only to send tribute and troops when called.

The Suren clan, one of the seven great noble houses of Parthia, seems to have had particular responsibility for the eastern frontier. A Suren general destroyed Crassus at Carrhae in 53 BCE - but his family's real work was in the east, policing Sistan, recruiting Saka cavalry, and keeping the road to India open. When Roman historians marveled at the thousand camel loads of arrows the Surenas deployed against Crassus, they were seeing, without knowing it, the logistical apparatus of a house that fought on the steppe frontier year in and year out.

The Sakas were never fully pacified. Periodic revolts and migrations kept the eastern marches unstable. But the Arsacid willingness to compromise - to let Saka be Saka inside the imperial frame - meant that the eastern frontier never collapsed the way the Roman Rhine did in the fifth century. When the Sasanians eventually replaced the Arsacids in 224 CE, they inherited an eastern frontier that was fractious but functional. That was a Parthian achievement whose value has rarely been acknowledged.

Trade and Diplomacy Across the Pamirs

Not all the traffic on the eastern frontier was hostile. Through the passes of the Hindu Kush and the high valleys of the Pamirs ran the great overland routes that later generations would call the Silk Road. The Parthians sat astride the western half of these roads, and they grew rich on them.

In 106 BCE, a Chinese embassy from the Han court of Emperor Wu reached the Parthian frontier. The Parthian king - probably Mithridates II - sent a cavalry escort of twenty thousand horsemen to meet them at the border, a display of power calibrated to impress the distant Chinese as much as to honor the guests. The embassy returned to Chang'an with ostrich eggs, jugglers from Alexandria, and reports of a vast and prosperous empire called Anxi, the Chinese name for Parthia derived from Arsaces himself.

For the next two centuries, Chinese silk flowed west through Parthian hands, and Parthian middlemen grew wealthy on the markup. The Romans, who craved silk and paid outrageous prices for it, never managed to buy it direct. A Chinese envoy named Gan Ying, sent west in 97 CE to establish contact with Rome, got as far as the Persian Gulf before Parthian officials talked him out of continuing, warning of three-year sea voyages and malevolent ocean spirits. The Parthians had no intention of letting their two greatest customers cut them out.

Diplomacy across the Pamirs was not only about silk. The Arsacids exchanged envoys with the Kushans, sometimes fighting them and sometimes allying with them against common enemies. They maintained relationships with the Saka dynasts of Sistan and with the Indo-Parthian kings at Taxila. The eastern Parthian court at cities like Merv and Hecatompylos was a polyglot place where Bactrian, Sogdian, Saka, and Indian traders and ambassadors mingled.

The archaeology bears this out. Parthian coins turn up in hoards across Central Asia. Chinese lacquerware and bronze mirrors appear in Parthian graves. Roman glass traveled east, Indian gems came west, and through it all the Arsacid customs officials took their percentage. It is one of the reasons the empire lasted as long as it did. A state that controls the tolls on the world's richest trade corridor can survive a great deal - lost battles, dynastic feuds, even the occasional Roman sack of its capital.

The Parthian East in Buddhist Sources

There is one more place to look for the Parthian east, and it is the least obvious: the Buddhist canon. Among the earliest translators of Buddhist scripture into Chinese were monks with unmistakably Iranian names, men who had come to the Han court from the Parthian world to the west.

The most famous was An Shigao, who arrived at the Chinese capital of Luoyang in 148 CE. His surname, An, was the Chinese abbreviation for

Anxi - Parthia. Tradition held that he was a Parthian prince who had renounced his throne to become a monk, traveling east through the Kushan lands and on to China, where he translated dozens of Buddhist texts into Chinese and founded one of the most influential translation lineages in East Asian religious history.

Whether An Shigao was really a prince is uncertain; the story has the flavor of hagiography. But his Parthian origin is firmly attested, and he was not alone. Other monks of Parthian background - An Xuan, An Fajin - appear in the early records of Chinese Buddhism. Sogdians and Kushans came too, but the Parthian presence was substantial and early. These men had learned Buddhism in the cosmopolitan cities of the Kushan and Indo-Parthian worlds, where monasteries flourished under royal patronage, and had carried it further east.

This is a dimension of Parthian history that classical sources cannot show us. To the Romans, Parthia was a military enemy and a source of luxury goods. To the Buddhists of Gandhara and Luoyang, it was a land from which learned monks came, fluent in several languages, bringing texts and ideas. The Arsacid empire, so often caricatured as a purely feudal and warlike state, was in fact porous enough at its eastern margins to produce scholars who could function in the intellectual world of Han China.

The eastern frontier was not only a zone of war but a zone of transmission. Ideas moved with the silk. Religions crossed the passes in the baggage of merchants and monks. And somewhere in that movement, a Parthian became a Chinese Buddhist saint.

Analysis

The Arsacids are usually judged by their wars with Rome, and by that measure they did magnificently. But the eastern frontier tells a different and arguably more important story. It was in the east that Parthia suffered its worst defeats - the loss of Bactria, the deaths of Phraates II and Artabanus I, the hemorrhage of territory to the Kushans. And it was in the east that Parthia showed its greatest administrative creativity, absorbing Saka populations, tolerating Indo-Parthian cousins, and taxing the Silk Road without strangling it.

The contrast with Rome is instructive. Rome's frontier policy ran on incorporation or exclusion - citizens or barbarians, nothing in between. The Parthian system allowed for gradations: fully imperial provinces, semi-autonomous satrapies, allied kingdoms, vassal clans, and trade partners of equal rank. It was messier, but it was also more durable on a frontier where steppe pressure never stopped. The Arsacids lost battles in the east, but they did not lose the frontier. That distinction mattered.

Quick Summary

- Parthia's eastern frontier, not its western one, caused its greatest military disasters, including the deaths of two kings in the 120s BCE.
- Bactria, the richest eastern province, was lost to Yuezhi and Saka nomads in the late second century BCE and became the heartland of the Kushan Empire.
- The Kushans, unified under Kanishka in the early second century CE, became a rival superpower that the Arsacids could neither conquer nor ignore.
- The Indo-Parthian kingdom of Gondophares (c. 19-46 CE) ruled the Indus valley with Arsacid political forms, independent of Ctesiphon.
- Saka migrations were absorbed through settlement in Sakastan (modern Sistan), managed largely by the noble house of Suren.
- Parthian control of the western Silk Road brought enormous wealth and allowed the Arsacids to keep Rome and China from trading directly.

- Parthian Buddhist monks like An Shigao carried scripture to Han China, revealing an eastern frontier of intellectual as well as military exchange.

The Arsacids are often called the forgotten empire, and nowhere is that forgetting more complete than on their eastern marches. The Roman sources that dominate our image of Parthia had no interest in what happened beyond the Iranian plateau. Yet it was there, in the high valleys of the Hindu Kush and the dry plains of Sistan, that the empire was tested most severely and adapted most inventively. Long after the Arsacid throne fell to the Sasanians in 224 CE, the patterns set on that frontier - of Iranian aristocracies ruling non-Iranian populations, of silk tolls and Buddhist monks, of cousin kingdoms in the Punjab - would shape Central Asia for a thousand years. The riders of the forgotten empire rode east as well as west, and the dust they raised is still settling.

For centuries the two-front empire had held. Arsacid kings absorbed Roman invasions in the west, bargained with Kushans and steppe confederations in the east, and let the internal coalition of noble houses renew itself through its usual grim rituals. The system was not elegant, but it worked. By the opening of the third century, though, the renewals were producing less and less. The noble houses were restive, the treasury thin, the succession exhausted by its own habits. The cracks that had always been in the crown began, at last, to widen.

Chapter 15:

Cracks in the Crown

In the year 216 CE, two men minted coins claiming to be King of Kings of the Parthians. They were brothers. Neither would rule long enough to repair the damage their quarrel had done.

The Arsacid house had survived civil wars before. It had endured defeat by Trajan, humiliation under Lucius Verus, the sack of Ctesiphon more than once. Each time it rose again, as if the dynasty were animated by some stubborn refusal to die. But the early third century presented something different - not a single catastrophic blow but a slow accumulation of them. A broken royal family. A treacherous Roman emperor. Frontier wars that drained silver from the treasury faster than the caravans could replace it. Great houses whose loyalty had curdled into indifference. And, in a quiet corner of the southwest, a governor whose ambitions the court in Ctesiphon had entirely failed to notice. What follows traces those converging pressures through the last two decades of Arsacid rule, from the dynastic split of 213 to the dust of Hormozdgan in 224, where a five-century empire ended in a single afternoon.

Vologases VI and Artabanus IV: A Dynasty Divided

Vologases VI came to the throne in 208 CE and, for about five years, ruled without serious challenge. Then, in 213, his brother Artabanus IV raised his own banner. What began as a family dispute hardened into a geographical partition. Vologases clung to Ctesiphon and the western heartlands along the Tigris. Artabanus seized Media and the Iranian plateau - the old Arsacid homeland, richer in cavalry, closer to the nobles who mattered.

The Parthian system had always tolerated a degree of royal competition. Fathers, sons, uncles, and cousins had fought over the diadem for centuries, and the empire's loose federal structure absorbed these quarrels the way a body absorbs minor fevers. Kings rose, kings fell; the great houses - Suren, Karen, Mihran - adjusted their allegiances and the wheel kept turning. This time, however, the quarrel did not resolve.

Numismatic evidence tells the story with mute precision. Vologases VI kept striking coins from his mint at Seleucia-Ctesiphon as late as 221 or 222, long after he had ceased to command armies capable of defending his claim. Artabanus, meanwhile, issued his own coinage from the east, and by 216 the Romans were treating him - not his brother - as the de facto Great King. Two monetary systems, two chancelleries, two courts of petitioners waiting to kiss a royal hand. For a frontier governor deciding whose tax demands to honor, such ambiguity was an invitation to pay neither.

The split also fractured the military. Parthian armies were coalitions. The King of Kings summoned the feudal levies of the great houses, and those houses then decided, case by case, how much of their strength to commit. A contested throne meant contested summonses. A noble who sent his cataphracts to fight for Artabanus in Media could not also send them to hold the Euphrates line against Rome. Neither brother could bring the empire's full weight to bear on any single problem, because the empire was no longer a single thing.

Personal details about the two kings are scarce - a recurring frustration with late Arsacid history, since the Parthians left almost no narrative sources of their own and the Roman historians were losing interest by this period. We know Artabanus was the more energetic of the two, that he commanded genuine respect among the Iranian nobility, and that he was capable, as events would shortly prove, of fielding armies that could bloody Roman legions. Vologases remains shadowy. He may have been the elder; he may simply have been less willing to retire gracefully. Whatever drove him to keep minting coins in a capital he barely controlled, that refusal cost the dynasty dearly.

The deeper problem was structural. An empire that could survive one rival king could not easily survive a rival king who refused to lose. Every month of stalemate taught the great houses that the center no longer held. Every month taught ambitious provincial governors - men like Ardashir, son of Papak, in faraway Fars - that the sky might not fall if they began to act on their own authority. The Arsacid state in 216 was still vast, still wealthy, still formidable on paper. In practice, it was a coalition whose chairman had lost the room.

Caracalla's Treachery and the Battle of Nisibis

Rome smelled the weakness. The emperor Caracalla, who had already murdered his own brother Geta to secure sole rule, fancied himself a second Alexander and looked east for glory. The Parthian civil war offered an opening no Roman emperor could refuse.

His opening move was diplomatic - and grotesque. Caracalla proposed marriage to a daughter of Artabanus IV, framing the union as a grand reconciliation of the two empires. Their children, he suggested, would inherit a world state stretching from Britain to India. Artabanus, according to the Greek historian Herodian, was skeptical but eventually consented. A wedding party was arranged on Parthian soil. Caracalla arrived with his army.

What happened next was a massacre. When the Parthian guests had gathered, unarmed and celebratory, Roman soldiers fell on them. Artabanus escaped - just - and rode east burning with a fury that would shortly be paid back in Roman blood. Whether the story is true in every detail or embroidered in the telling, something of the kind clearly occurred in 216. Caracalla's campaign that year involved a march deep into Media, the desecration of Arsacid royal tombs at Arbela, and a general policy of calculated terror. The treachery confirmed, for the Parthian nobility, that Rome was not a partner but a predator.

Caracalla did not live to face the consequences. In April 217, while stopping to relieve himself beside a road near Carrhae - the same ghost-haunted ground where Crassus had died two and a half centuries earlier - he was stabbed to death by one of his own guardsmen. His successor, Macrinus, a career bureaucrat with no military reputation, inherited a war he had not chosen and an enemy he could not appease.

Artabanus came for him. In the summer of 217 the Parthian army, hungry for vengeance, crossed into Roman Mesopotamia and met the legions outside Nisibis. The battle lasted three days. Ancient accounts describe a grinding affair in which Parthian cataphracts and horse archers wore down the Roman infantry while camel-mounted troops - a tactical wrinkle Macrinus had not expected - spread confusion in the Roman rear. By the third evening, both sides had suffered heavily, but the Romans had suffered more. Macrinus asked for terms.

The terms were expensive. Rome paid Artabanus an indemnity of roughly two hundred million sesterces - one of the largest sums a Roman emperor ever handed to a foreign power - along with the return of prisoners and booty taken in Caracalla's raid. On the ledger of empires, Nisibis was a Parthian victory. Artabanus rode home with gold, prestige, and the satisfaction of having humbled the killers of his kin.

Victory came at a price the accountants could not calculate. The war had consumed men, horses, and silver that the Arsacid state, already fractured between two kings, could not easily replace. The great houses that had answered Artabanus's summons now expected rewards. The eastern frontier had been thinned to staff the western one. And Vologases VI, still stubbornly minting coins at Ctesiphon, still refused to concede. Artabanus had beaten Rome. He had not beaten his brother, and he had not beaten the deeper disease of his dynasty.

Economic Strain and Noble Disaffection

An empire runs on silver, and by the 220s Parthian silver was thinning on the tongue. The drachms struck in the last Arsacid decades show a measurable decline in weight and purity compared to the confident issues of the first century CE. Coins are honest witnesses. When a king debases his currency, he is telling his subjects that the treasury cannot meet the obligations the court has already incurred.

Several pressures converged. The Silk Road trade, that long artery of Parthian wealth, had been disrupted repeatedly - by plague in the 160s, by campaigning armies tearing up the Mesopotamian plain, by the growing habit of Roman merchants and Kushan middlemen of routing luxury goods around Parthian territory rather than through it. Ctesiphon had been sacked three times in a century: by Trajan in 116, by Avidius Cassius in 165, by Septimius Severus in 198. Each sack stripped the capital of bullion, artisans, and the intangible confidence that makes capitals function.

The Nisibis indemnity of 217 should have replenished the treasury. In practice, much of it went to the nobles whose levies had fought the war, not into state coffers. This was the Arsacid bargain in miniature: the king summoned the great houses, the great houses won the battle, and the king paid them for their trouble. It worked when wars were short and booty plentiful. It worked less well when a war against Rome had to be financed by a court that also needed those nobles to hold the eastern frontier, police the caravan routes, and - most urgently - to not join the rival king across the plateau.

That rival king was the deeper drain. A divided succession meant that every noble house could now play a double game, extracting concessions from both brothers. Estates were enlarged. Tax exemptions were granted. Royal lands were quietly absorbed into noble ones. The Arsacid crown had always been first among equals rather than an autocracy; but by the 220s, the first among equals was beginning to look less like a king and more like an overextended landlord.

Noble disaffection was not, in most cases, outright rebellion. It was something more corrosive: indifference. When a provincial governor in Fars began to refuse royal orders, when he killed neighboring vassals and annexed their lands, when he crowned himself king in his own city - the news traveled to Ctesiphon and to Artabanus's court, and no one could spare the troops to intervene. The great houses shrugged. Fars was far away. Their own estates were closer. Their own quarrels more pressing.

A religious fraying compounded the political one. Zoroastrian priestly communities, particularly in the south and east, had long felt that the Arsacids - with their Greek inscriptions, their Hellenized court culture, their comparatively loose patronage of the Mazdean faith - were insufficiently Iranian. This was not quite a grievance that could topple a dynasty on its own. But it was a grievance that could supply moral cover to whoever did. When Ardashir of Fars began to wrap his ambitions in the language of religious restoration, he was reaching for an idiom already prepared for him.

By 222, the Arsacid state was not yet broken. But it was hollow in ways its enemies had noticed and its defenders had not. A single hard push, applied at the right angle, would be enough.

The House of Sasan in Persis

In the hill country of Fars - the ancient Persis, homeland of Cyrus and Darius - an obscure family had been quietly rising. Their founder, or at least their genealogical anchor, was a priest named Sasan, about whom almost nothing is known. The later Sasanian dynasty would claim him as an ancestor of royal Achaemenid blood, but such claims are the common currency of dynasts looking for legitimacy. What can be said with confidence is that by the late second century, Sasan's descendants had acquired custody of the fire temple of Anahita at Istakhr, near the ruins of Persepolis. A fire temple was a political as well as a religious institution - a node of local authority, a magnet for patronage, a platform.

Sasan's son Papak, sometimes written Babak, made the family's first move into hard politics. Around the turn of the third century he overthrew the local Parthian vassal-king of Istakhr, a man named Gochihr, and installed himself in his place. This was not, technically, rebellion against the Arsacids. Papak kept paying his taxes and sending the ritual courtesies to Ctesiphon. He had simply replaced one vassal with another - himself. The distinction mattered, because it allowed the coup to pass almost unnoticed in an empire preoccupied with civil war and Roman invasion.

Papak had several sons. The eldest, Shapur, appears to have been the designated heir. The younger, Ardashir, had been placed in charge of a minor fortress town called Darabgird. Ardashir did not remain minor for long. He was, by every measure we can reconstruct, a man of formidable drive - ruthless, methodical, and possessed of a strategic patience rare in an age of impatient princes.

When Papak died, Ardashir moved against his own brother. Shapur, according to the later Sasanian sources, conveniently died when a piece of masonry fell on him at the ancestral palace; whether by accident or arrangement, the sources do not say, and the sources are not neutral. Ardashir became sole ruler of Fars around 208 CE - the same year, by coincidence or by design, that Vologases VI was enthroned in Ctesiphon.

From Darabgird and Istakhr, Ardashir began a campaign of systematic expansion that has few parallels in ancient history for its sheer cold-blooded clarity. He absorbed Kerman. He took Isfahan. He reduced the petty kingdoms of the Persian Gulf coast and the Elamite hills. At each stage he offered the local dynast a choice: submission or death. Many submitted. Those who did not were killed, and their lands added to his.

Throughout this process he continued, nominally, to be a Parthian vassal. Coins from the period show him wearing a distinctive tall cap decorated with a star and crescent, a deliberate signal of independence, but the legends remained cautious. He was building an empire inside another empire, and he understood that premature provocation could invite the one response Ctesiphon might still be capable of: a massed royal army sent south to crush him while he was still consolidating.

Artabanus IV, belatedly alarmed, ordered his vassal in Khuzestan to deal with the upstart. Ardashir defeated him. Artabanus ordered another vassal to try. Ardashir defeated him too. By about 220 CE, the governor of Fars had become the most successful warlord in Iran, and the King of Kings was running out of subordinates willing to march against him. The time for cautious coinage was over. Ardashir began to style himself king in his own right, and the confrontation the Arsacid court had postponed for a decade could be postponed no longer.

The Road to Hormozdgan

Artabanus IV was not a weak king. He had beaten Caracalla and humbled Macrinus. His cavalry was among the finest in the world. Had he marched against Ardashir in 215, or 218, or even 221, the weight of the Arsacid state would probably have been too much for the upstart from Fars. He did not march. He was busy - with Rome, with his brother, with the politics of holding together a coalition that no longer wanted to be held.

By the time he did march, in the spring of 224, Ardashir had conquered most of southern and western Iran. The two armies converged on a plain whose exact location is disputed - the sources call it Hormozdgan, and it lay somewhere in Khuzestan or the neighboring mountains, near a river whose course has since shifted. What is not disputed is what happened there.

Artabanus brought the traditional Parthian host: cataphracts in scale armor, horse archers, allied contingents from the great houses that had still answered his summons. Ardashir brought an army that looked, on the surface, similar - the military technology of Iran had not changed in a generation - but was structured differently. His cavalry answered to a single chain of command. His nobles had been selected by him, promoted by him, and owed everything to him. There was no coalition to fracture under pressure.

The battle, according to later Sasanian tradition, ended in a duel. Ardashir and Artabanus met in single combat in the midst of the general engagement, and Ardashir killed the King of Kings with his own hand. Whether that is history or dynastic theater, the outcome is certain: Artabanus died on the field, his army dissolved, and the last serious Arsacid resistance ended with him.

Vologases VI, still minting his coins somewhere in the west, held out for perhaps another four or five years before vanishing entirely from the record. He is the last Arsacid whose name we know. Nearly five centuries of Parthian rule - from Arsaces I's first raid into Parthava in 247 BCE to the dust of Hormozdgan - ended not with a conquest by Rome, the enemy everyone had expected, but by a governor from Fars whose family history the Ctesiphon court had never bothered to learn.

Analysis

Why did the Arsacids fall? The simplest answer is that they ran out of time to fix what they had always known was broken. The federal structure that had made the empire resilient in its middle centuries - great houses as partners rather than subjects, vassal kings as local managers rather than appointed governors - also made it impossible to centralize quickly when centralization was what the moment demanded. Rome had been pushing the Parthians toward a more unified state for two hundred years. The Parthians, understandably, had resisted the transformation because every step toward it required the great houses to surrender power they had no reason to surrender.

Ardashir's genius was to build that unified state not by reforming the old one but by growing a new one alongside it, in a province too peripheral to attract Ctesiphon's attention until it was too late. When the two systems finally met at Hormozdgan, the contest was between a coalition and a command, and the command won.

The lesson is not that Parthian federalism was doomed. It had survived Roman invasions, plague, civil wars, and sacked capitals for nearly half a millennium. The lesson is narrower and sadder: a system built to absorb many small shocks cannot always absorb one sustained one. Two rival kings for a decade, a draining war with Rome, a debased currency, a rising warlord in the south - any one of these the Arsacids could have managed. All of them at once, they could not.

Quick Summary

- In 213 CE the Parthian throne split between the brothers Vologases VI and Artabanus IV; the dynastic war continued for roughly a decade with no resolution.
- In 216 Caracalla lured Artabanus with a false marriage proposal and massacred his wedding party, triggering a Parthian war of vengeance.
- Artabanus defeated Macrinus at Nisibis in 217 and extracted a massive indemnity - a tactical victory that did nothing to heal the empire's internal fractures.
- Parthian silver coinage declined in weight and purity through the late period, reflecting trade disruption, repeated sacks of Ctesiphon, and the costs of a divided state.

- The great houses grew increasingly indifferent to the Arsacid crown, extracting concessions from both rival kings while consolidating their own estates.
- In Fars, the family of Sasan rose through Papak's seizure of Istakhr and then Ardashir's methodical conquest of neighboring kingdoms, beginning around 208 CE.
- By 220, Ardashir had defeated every vassal Artabanus sent against him and openly claimed kingship.
- At the Battle of Hormozdgan in 224, Artabanus IV was killed, ending five centuries of Arsacid rule and opening the Sasanian era.

The Parthians had ruled an empire for longer than Rome would ever rule one in the west. Their collapse produced no lasting dirge because their successors, the Sasanians, had every reason to bury them. Ardashir and his heirs wrote the histories, struck the coins, and carved the reliefs that would define how Iran remembered its own past. In those retellings the Arsacids became shadowy, quarrelsome, vaguely un-Iranian - a dynasty best forgotten. But the empire they built had shaped the Silk Road, humbled Rome, preserved the bones of Iranian kingship through five chaotic centuries, and made possible the very state that would erase them. The crown cracked at Hormozdgan. What had worn it first deserves to be remembered.

A dynasty that had survived Trajan and Verus and its own murderous princes would not be undone by a single battlefield defeat, except that, in the end, it was. The cracks in the crown narrowed the field of possibilities until a minor king from Fars could ride onto a dusty plain with a realistic hope of unseating the King of Kings. What happened at Hormozdgan in 224 CE took less than a day and closed five centuries. The battle itself, and the man who won it, deserve their own reckoning.

Chapter 16:

Hormozdgan, 224 CE: The End of the Arsacids

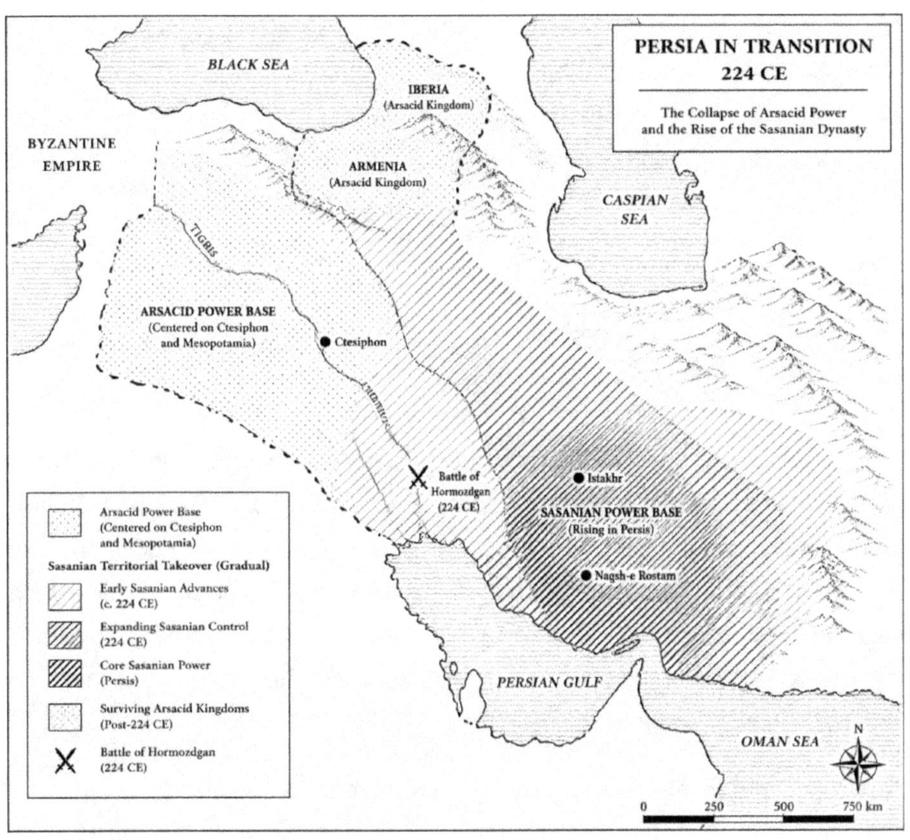

The End of an Empire: Hormozdgan and the Sasanian Rise, 224 CE

Five centuries. That is how long the Arsacid banner had flown over the Iranian plateau when, on the morning of 28 April 224, a minor king from the south rode out onto a dusty plain to end it all.

The battle that followed barely lasted a day. Yet it closed a dynasty older than the Roman Empire, older than the Han in China, and older than most of the gods still worshipped along the Silk Road. The man who won it, Ardashir son of Papak, would take the ancient title *shahanshah* - King of Kings - and build upon the Parthian bones a new empire that would haunt Rome for four more centuries. The man who lost it, Artabanus IV, vanished into the red dust of Hormozdgan, taking with him the last flicker of a Parthian world that had stretched from the Euphrates to the Indus. What follows is an account of how a provincial rebel from Fars toppled a superpower, why the Parthian state proved so brittle at the top yet so stubborn at the bottom, and how the memory of the Arsacids outlived their throne by a very long time indeed.

Ardashir's Rise in Fars

The province of Persis - Fars in modern Persian - was the heartland of the old Achaemenid kings. Cyrus and Darius had built their tombs there. Their ruined palaces at Persepolis still stood, blackened by Alexander's fire but legible to anyone who cared to read the inscriptions. For nearly five hundred years under Parthian rule, Fars had been a quiet place, governed by local dynasts who paid tribute to the Arsacid court in Ctesiphon and otherwise kept their heads down.

Ardashir came from this quiet. His grandfather Sasan, the family's eponym, had been a priestly figure associated with the temple of Anahita at Istakhr, near the ruins of Persepolis itself. His father Papak had been a local king of modest standing. When Papak died around 208, Ardashir - already governor of the small town of Darabgird - moved with striking speed. He seized Istakhr, killed or sidelined his rivals within his own family, and declared himself king of Persis.

For nearly a decade he worked outward from that base. One by one, the petty kingdoms of southern Iran fell to him: Kerman, Isfahan, the Elymaean highlands, the shores of the Persian Gulf. He built new cities, or rebuilt old ones, with names that advertised his ambition: Ardashir-Khwarrah, *the Glory of Ardashir*. He struck coins in his own name, wearing a distinctive crown that broke sharply from Parthian fashion. And he began to gather around himself a court culture that consciously reached past the Arsacids to the deeper Iranian past - to Cyrus, to Darius, to the fire altars of the old Zoroastrian priesthood.

This was no ordinary rebellion. The Parthians had dealt with breakaway satraps before; the empire's history was a long chronicle of such revolts, most of them crushed, a few bought off. What made Ardashir different was his program. He did not simply want to carve out a kingdom. He wanted to replace the very idea of the Arsacid state with something older and, to his mind, more authentically Iranian.

The Arsacids, despite their long tenure, had always carried a faint whiff of the outsider. Their founder Arsaces had been a chief of the Parni, a nomadic people from the steppes beyond the Caspian. Their court spoke Parthian, a northern dialect. Their religion was Iranian but eclectic, tolerant of Greek gods, of Semitic cults, of the Mesopotamian shrines they had inherited. For a southern Persian steeped in the traditions of Fars, all this looked like a long interruption - a half-millennium detour between the fall of Darius III and the restoration that Ardashir now intended to lead.

By 216, Ardashir's armies were pushing into Khuzestan, on the very doorstep of the Parthian royal heartland. The court at Ctesiphon could no longer ignore him. The trouble was that the court at Ctesiphon was, at that moment, at war with itself.

The Final Campaigns of Artabanus IV

Artabanus IV had inherited a poisoned throne. His brother Vologases VI held Ctesiphon and the western provinces; Artabanus, ruling from Media and the east, spent the better part of a decade fighting his own sibling in a slow, grinding civil war. Only around 216 did Artabanus manage to establish clear control over most of the empire, and even then Vologases continued to mint coins from Seleucia-on-the-Tigris, a stubborn rival who would outlive Artabanus himself.

No sooner had Artabanus won his dynastic war than Rome came knocking. The emperor Caracalla, casting himself as a new Alexander, arrived in the east in 216 demanding the hand of Artabanus's daughter. The demand was less about marriage than humiliation: Caracalla wanted to unite the empires on Roman terms. Artabanus refused, Caracalla invaded, and Roman legions pushed through Media sacking royal tombs at Arbela. Then, in April 217, Caracalla was murdered by his own officers on a roadside near Carrhae - the same plain where Crassus had died nearly three centuries before.

Artabanus struck back hard. His armies met the new emperor Macrinus at Nisibis in 217 in one of the largest battles fought between Rome and Parthia. The Romans bought their way out with an enormous indemnity, reported by Cassius Dio at two hundred million sesterces. On paper, it was a Parthian victory. In practice, Artabanus had spent the blood and treasure of an empire already exhausted by civil war, on a campaign whose gains were purely monetary.

He never had time to recover. The armies he needed to deal with Ardashir were the same armies that had bled at Nisibis. The nobility whose loyalty he needed had spent years watching the Arsacid brothers tear the realm apart. And crucially, many of the old clans of the east - the Suren, the Karen, the Mihran - had local reasons to hedge their bets. Some would ultimately fight for Ardashir. Others simply stayed home.

Between 220 and 224, Artabanus campaigned south, trying to cork the bottle before Ardashir burst out of Fars entirely. There were skirmishes, inconclusive engagements, small reversals. Ardashir fought three battles against Artabanus's vassals and subordinate commanders before the main encounter, and won them all. Each victory tipped another fence-sitting noble house into the Sasanian camp. Each defeat peeled another regiment away from the Arsacid standard.

By the spring of 224, Artabanus had no more time. He gathered the forces still loyal to him - a large army, by the standards of the age, drawing on Media, on the eastern marches, and on what remained of the royal guard - and marched south to finish the upstart. He chose the ground with some care, but Ardashir, as it turned out, had chosen it first.

Exactly where Hormozdgan lay is disputed; the likeliest location is a plain in the borderlands between Khuzestan and Isfahan, somewhere along the routes that funnelled armies between the plateau and the lowland. What is clear is that Artabanus arrived expecting to crush a provincial rebel with superior numbers and centuries of royal legitimacy behind him. He found instead a commander who had been preparing for this day for fifteen years.

The Battle of Hormozdgan

Ardashir had reached the plain first and fortified it. His men dug a defensive ditch along his chosen front, channeling any Parthian charge into killing ground of his own design. He positioned his forces - perhaps ten thousand cavalry, heavily armored, supported by lighter horse and infantry - on rising ground with water at his back and the sun, when the day came, in a direction that favored his archers. Every Iranian commander since the Achaemenids had known that cavalry battles on open plain turned on mobility and terrain. Ardashir, fighting on ground he had picked and prepared, had stripped both advantages from his enemy before the first arrow flew.

Artabanus arrived with a larger force but a crucial disadvantage. His men had marched hard to reach the field; Ardashir's had rested. His numbers, meant to overwhelm, crowded together in a space too narrow to exploit them. And his cavalry, the celebrated Parthian combination of horse archers and cataphracts, needed room to maneuver - room the ditch and the terrain denied them.

The battle opened, as Parthian battles always did, with arrows. Waves of mounted archers sprayed the Sasanian lines and were answered in kind. But the famous Parthian tactic - feigned flight followed by the devastating backward shot - required space to run, and there was none. When Artabanus committed his cataphracts, the armored heavy cavalry that had shattered Roman legions at Carrhae, they met Ardashir's equally heavy horsemen on ground that allowed no flanking maneuver.

Accounts of what happened next are more legend than history. The Sasanian tradition, preserved centuries later in the *Karnamag i Ardashir*, described the battle in terms drawn straight from epic: Ardashir and Artabanus seeking each other out, a personal combat, the King of Kings cut down by the rising challenger. His son Shapur - the future Shapur I, who would one day capture a Roman emperor alive - fought beside him. In one version, it was Shapur himself who struck the decisive blow against Dad-windad, Artabanus's chief secretary, a man whose name survives only because of the manner of his death.

What is historically clear is the outcome. Artabanus IV was killed on the field. His army broke, scattering northward toward Media. Dad-windad was taken prisoner and executed on Ardashir's orders - not out of cruelty, but as a message: the Arsacid administrative machinery, not merely its royal family, was to be replaced. The chief secretary was the living symbol of the old bureaucracy, and his death closed that office as thoroughly as Artabanus's closed the throne.

The battle itself may have lasted only hours. Its consequences were immediate. Ardashir rode straight north toward Ctesiphon, where he would formally crown himself *shahanshah*, King of Kings - a title deliberately reaching back past the Arsacids to the Achaemenid Darius. The coinage changed. The court language began to shift from Parthian to Middle Persian. The fire temples of Fars rose in prestige, and the priestly class that had nurtured Ardashir's rise began the long work of codifying what would become orthodox Zoroastrianism.

On that plain in southern Iran, one empire had ended and another had begun. But endings in the ancient world were rarely as clean as their victors wished.

The Last Arsacids and the Kingdom of Armenia

Ardashir was a thorough man, but he was not an omnipresent one. In the months and years after Hormozdgan, he marched through province after province, taking cities, reducing fortresses, compelling nobles to submit. Some resisted bitterly. Hatra, the caravan city in the western desert, held out until 240, when Shapur finally broke it. Other cities surrendered and had their walls pulled down. A new dynasty was being written, one wall at a time.

Meanwhile, the Arsacid family did not simply vanish. Vologases VI, Artabanus's long-time rival, continued to strike coins at Seleucia at least into 228, four years after Hormozdgan - a ghost king minting money for a kingdom that no longer existed. Other Arsacid princes fled. Some went east, to the courts of the small kingdoms along the edges of the former empire. Some went north.

North meant Armenia. And in Armenia, the Arsacids were already at home.

Since the first century CE, Armenia had been ruled by a cadet branch of the Parthian royal house - an arrangement hammered out in the long diplomatic wars with Rome and formalized under Nero. When the main line fell at

Hormozdgan, the Armenian Arsacids did not fall with them. They ruled on from their capital at Vagharshapat, and they regarded the Sasanians not as legitimate heirs but as usurpers who had murdered their kinsman.

This grudge would shape the politics of the Near East for the next two centuries. The Armenian Arsacids kept the old dynasty's memory alive, kept its coinage circulating, kept its claims pressed. When Sasanian armies marched north, Armenian kings resisted. When Rome offered alliance against the new Persian empire, Armenia listened. The Sasanians, for their part, could never quite let Armenia be - it was an Arsacid remnant on their doorstep, a reminder that their victory had been incomplete.

The Armenian branch outlasted the Sasanians who had overthrown their cousins. They ruled until 428, when internal quarrels and Sasanian pressure finally extinguished their kingdom - more than two centuries after Hormozdgan. By then Rome itself had split, the western half was collapsing, and the Sasanians were locked in the death-struggle with Byzantium that would leave both exhausted before the Arab conquests. Yet in the mountains of eastern Anatolia, an Arsacid king had sat on a throne the whole time.

Other survivals followed a similar pattern. In the Caucasus, the kingdom of Iberia (modern Georgia) maintained an Arsacid-descended dynasty into the second century. The noble houses of Parthia itself - the Suren, the Karen, the Mihran, the Ispahbudhan - did not disappear either. They became the great aristocratic clans of the Sasanian Empire, reluctant partners whom the new dynasty could never quite subjugate and never quite do without. When the Sasanians themselves fell, seven Parthian clans would still be on the field.

Why the Parthian State Fell - and Why Slowly

Ardashir's victory at Hormozdgan was swift. The Parthian state's decline was not. The Arsacid system had worked, in its fashion, for half a millennium. Its failure was not a matter of a single lost battle.

Structural weaknesses had been visible for generations. The Arsacids ruled a confederation rather than a centralized state, relying on great noble houses and client kings whose loyalty was personal and conditional. This had been a strength in the empire's youth, when it allowed rapid expansion and local legitimacy. It became a weakness as the Roman threat grew, because federations are slower to mobilize and harder to tax than centralized kingdoms. Every major Roman war - Trajan's invasion in 115, Lucius Verus's in 165, Septimius Severus's in 197, Caracalla's in 216 - had exposed the limits of what the Arsacid system could absorb.

Succession was the other chronic ailment. The Parthian throne passed by a combination of patrilineal descent and noble acclamation, which in practice meant that every royal death opened the door to civil war. The last seventy years of Arsacid rule were a near-continuous contest between rival brothers, uncles, nephews, and pretenders. Artabanus's decade-long struggle with Vologases VI was only the final installment of a very long series.

Economic strain compounded both problems. The great Silk Road trade that had enriched Parthia for centuries had been disrupted by war, by plague - the Antonine Plague of the 160s killed untold numbers across the Iranian world - and by the gradual shift of trade routes. Roman sackings of Ctesiphon and Seleucia stripped the empire of wealth that was never fully recovered.

So when Ardashir rose, he rose into a system ready to crack. But consider what he did not change. The Sasanian army kept the Parthian mix of cataphracts and horse archers. The Sasanian nobility was, in many cases, the same Parthian nobility under a new master. The administrative language shifted from Parthian to Middle Persian, but many of the administrative practices were inherited whole. Even the title *shahanshah*, though Ardashir traced it to the Achaemenids, had been used by late Arsacid kings too.

The Parthian state fell at Hormozdgan, but the Parthian world did not. It was absorbed, repurposed, and carried forward under a different banner. The riders on the plain were the same riders. The empire had changed hands, not character.

Quick Summary

- Ardashir I declared himself king of Persis around 208 CE and spent fifteen years conquering southern and central Iran before challenging the Arsacids directly.
- Artabanus IV reunified most of the Parthian Empire by 216 but was exhausted by civil war with his brother Vologases VI and by costly wars with Rome under Caracalla and Macrinus.
- At the Battle of Hormozdgan on 28 April 224, Ardashir's smaller force of roughly ten thousand cavalry used prepared ground and a defensive ditch to defeat Artabanus's larger army. Artabanus was killed; his chief secretary Dad-windad was executed.
- Ardashir took the title *shahanshah*, founded the Sasanian Empire, and began a systematic conquest of the remaining Parthian territories, culminating in the fall of Hatra in 240.
- The Arsacid dynasty survived in Armenia until 428 CE, and Arsacid-derived noble houses remained powerful within the Sasanian Empire itself.
- Parthian military tactics, aristocratic structures, and much administrative practice passed intact into the Sasanian system.
- The Arsacid state fell because of structural weaknesses - decentralized governance, contested succession, and economic strain - that had been accumulating for generations.

Five centuries of Parthian history ended in a single afternoon on a plain whose exact location we no longer know. Yet the empire that replaced the Arsacids would rule Iran for 427 years, fight Rome and then Byzantium to a standstill, and fall at last not to a Western army but to the Arab armies of a new faith. When that moment came, in the seventh century, the Sasanians looked back on Hormozdgan as their founding triumph. But they fought with Parthian cavalry, paid Parthian nobles, and lost to men who would soon be praying toward a city the Arsacids had never known. Empires rarely end cleanly. Sometimes they only change their names.

Hormozdgan ended a dynasty, but it did not end the civilization the Arsacids had built. The Sasanians fought with Parthian cavalry, paid Parthian nobles, and ruled through administrative habits their predecessors had perfected. What they would not do was credit them. The most consequential thing Ardashir's heirs did to the Arsacids was not defeat them on the battlefield but erase them from the record afterward, and that erasure is itself part of the Parthian story. How an empire of five centuries was forgotten, and how it is now being remembered, closes the book.

Chapter 17:

The Parthian Afterlife

No empire that lasts nearly five centuries should be easy to forget. Yet the Parthians very nearly vanished from the historical record, and the men who overthrew them were not about to help them be remembered.

When Ardashir I rode out of Persis in 224 CE and cut down the last Arsacid king, he inherited more than a throne. He inherited an archive, a priesthood, a court culture, and a memory - and he set about reshaping all of them. What followed was one of the most successful acts of political erasure in the ancient world. For nearly two thousand years, the Parthians would be remembered mostly as the people the Sasanians replaced, the shadowy enemy Roman generals chased across the Euphrates, the blank space on the map between Greece and China. Only in the last century, as archaeologists dug into the mounds of Nisa and Hatra and Dura-Europos, and as numismatists began to read the faces on Arsacid coins with fresh eyes, has the shape of the real empire begun to reappear. What follows concerns what was lost, what survived underground, and how the Parthians - long after they ceased to rule anything - continued to shape the world from Armenia to Rome to the poetry of medieval Iran.

Sasanian Propaganda and the Erasure of Memory

The Sasanians were the most effective revisionists of antiquity. Within a generation of Ardashir's victory, court scribes were at work on an official past in which the Parthians barely existed.

The pattern is visible in the great rock reliefs Ardashir commissioned at Naqsh-e Rustam and Firuzabad. In one, the new king receives the ring of kingship directly from the god Ahura Mazda; beneath the hooves of their horses, the vanquished enemy is the Parthian king Artabanus IV. The message is unambiguous. Legitimate kingship had passed from the Achaemenids - the dynasty of Cyrus and Darius - directly to the Sasanians, as if the four and a half centuries in between had been a regrettable interruption.

That interruption had a name in Sasanian historiography: the *muluk al-tawa'if*, the "kings of the tribes" or "petty kings." It was a term of contempt. In the version of Iranian history that the Sasanians standardized and that later passed into Arabic and Persian sources, the Arsacids were not a great imperial dynasty but a squabbling collection of warlords who had let Iran fall into fragments after the defeat of the Achaemenids by Alexander. The real story of Iran, in this telling, resumed only when Ardashir restored unity.

The erasure went deeper than rhetoric. Sasanian priests consolidated the Zoroastrian scriptures into an authorized canon, and the versions of religious history they transmitted marginalized the Parthian centuries. Court genealogies traced the new dynasty back to the ancient kings of Persis, skipping over the Arsacid age entirely. When the Sasanian chronicle tradition finally reached the great Persian epic of Ferdowsi, the *Shahnameh*, nearly eight centuries after Ardashir's victory, the Parthian period occupied perhaps twenty lines out of fifty thousand. Ferdowsi himself apologizes for the brevity: the records, he writes, simply do not exist.

They did not exist because they had been allowed to disappear. Arsacid royal archives, inscriptions, and dynastic histories were not systematically preserved. Coins - which the Sasanians could not easily destroy because they circulated in millions across Eurasia - became, ironically, the richest surviving source for Parthian chronology. The kings whose faces appear on those coins, bearded and diademed and looking out from the tetradrachms of Seleucia, would be identified and sequenced only by modern scholars working with catalogues and die studies. Many are still known only as "Unknown King I" or "Unknown King II."

The strange result is that a dynasty that ruled from the Euphrates to the Hindu Kush, that humiliated Crassus at Carrhae and held Mark Antony at bay and negotiated with Augustus as an equal, left less written memory than a minor Hellenistic city-state. The Sasanians had done their work well. It would take modern archaeology, two millennia later, to undo it.

The Parthian Noble Houses Under New Masters

The Parthians did not actually vanish in 224 CE. The great noble clans - the Suren, the Karen, the Mihran, the Ispahbudhan - bent the knee to Ardashir and kept their estates, their private armies, and their ancient privileges. The Sasanians had won a dynastic war, not a social revolution.

This was partly a matter of necessity. The Parthian political order had always been decentralized, a confederation of vassal kings and landed aristocrats bound to the Arsacid throne by personal loyalty rather than bureaucratic control. Ardashir could dispose of the Arsacid family, but he could not administer Iran without the very magnates who had administered it for the Arsacids. So he co-opted them.

The Suren clan, whose ancestors had produced the general who destroyed Crassus at Carrhae, continued to supply commanders and marzbans - frontier wardens - to Sasanian kings for the next four hundred years. The Karen held lands in Media and Nihavand through the entire Sasanian period. The Mihran produced some of the most formidable Sasanian generals, including the Bahram Chobin who very nearly seized the throne himself in the 590s CE. When the Arab armies broke through the Sasanian defenses in the 630s, the men who led the last Iranian resistance - Rustam at the battle of al-Qadisiyyah, the marzbans of Khurasan - carried the names of Parthian houses.

Parthian military technique survived with the Parthian aristocracy. The heavily armored cataphract, the mounted archer, the combined-arms tactics that had bled Roman legions dry - all of these became the core of the Sasanian way of war and, later, of early Islamic cavalry. Ceremonial court culture, with its hierarchies of ranks and its elaborate hunting rituals, drew heavily on Parthian precedent. Even the official language shifted only gradually. Middle Persian replaced Parthian in royal inscriptions, but Parthian remained a literary and administrative language in parts of the empire for generations.

There is a quiet irony here. The Sasanians insisted publicly that the Parthian centuries had been a period of weakness and decline. In practice, they staffed their armies with Parthian commanders, fought with Parthian weapons, and ruled over a terrain whose local power structures the Parthians had built. The dynasty had fallen; the class that had run the empire simply changed its allegiance and carried on.

The Legacy in Armenia, Georgia, and Central Asia

Beyond the Iranian plateau, the Arsacid name outlived the Parthian Empire itself - in some places by centuries.

Armenia is the clearest case. A cadet branch of the Arsacid family had ruled there since 54 CE, installed as part of a settlement with Rome, and it continued to rule after the main line in Ctesiphon was extinguished. The Armenian Arsacids held the throne until 428 CE, more than two hundred years after Ardashir's victory. They presided over one of the defining moments in Armenian history: the conversion of the kingdom to Christianity around 301 CE under Tiridates III, making Armenia the first officially Christian state in the world. The king who made that decision was a Parthian by blood, ruling from a court whose titles, ceremonies, and aristocratic structure were direct inheritances from Ctesiphon.

Armenian noble houses - the *nakharars* - were themselves often of Parthian origin or had intermarried with Parthian aristocracy. The Kamsarakan claimed descent from the Karen. The Mamikonian, who would dominate Armenian military life for centuries and produce the national hero Vardan, traced their origins, at least in legend, to the east. The Armenian feudal order that endured into the medieval period was, in its bones, a Parthian order.

Georgia tells a similar story. The kings of Iberia, the eastern Georgian kingdom, adopted Arsacid titles and married into Arsacid families. Georgian historical tradition preserves Parthian loanwords in its vocabulary of kingship and warfare, fossilized evidence of the centuries when Parthian power reached into the Caucasus.

Further east, the picture is more fragmented but no less striking. The Kushan Empire, which rose in what is now Afghanistan and northern India in the first and second centuries CE, absorbed heavy Parthian influence in its coinage, its titulature, and its court culture. The Indo-Parthian kingdom of Gondophares, ruling in the first century CE in the region around Taxila, was a direct political offshoot. Christian tradition remembers Gondophares as the king at whose court the apostle Thomas preached - a detail that, whatever its historical accuracy, testifies to how deeply the Parthian world extended into the imagination of late antiquity.

Along the Silk Road, Parthian merchants and the Parthian language had established themselves so firmly that the Sogdians, who inherited much of the east-west trade, worked within commercial and diplomatic conventions laid down in the Arsacid centuries. The Chinese dynastic histories, which called the Parthian realm Anxi - a transliteration of Arsaces - recorded Parthian embassies and Parthian goods long after the dynasty had fallen in the west. The Parthians had not simply ruled an empire; they had wired together a continent, and the wiring stayed in place long after the switchboard had changed hands.

What Rome Absorbed from Parthia

Rome's relationship with Parthia was officially one of hostility. Seven major wars, a string of humiliations at Carrhae and elsewhere, and a diplomatic rivalry that lasted three centuries left Roman writers with a vocabulary of contempt for everything Parthian - treacherous, effeminate, oriental, soft. Beneath the insults, however, Rome was quietly learning.

Military borrowing came first and ran deepest. The Parthian mounted archer, who could loose arrows while galloping away from pursuers, gave Latin a verb: *to parthianize*, to feign retreat. The "Parthian shot" entered European languages as both a tactic and a metaphor. More importantly, the cataphract - the fully armored lancer on an armored horse - entered the Roman order of battle. By the third century, Roman armies fielded their own *clibanarii* and *cataphractarii*, and the trend only accelerated under the later empire. The heavily armored Byzantine horseman, and ultimately the medieval European knight, traced a direct line of tactical descent from the plains of Parthia.

Roman diplomacy learned lessons too. After Carrhae in 53 BCE and the debacles that followed, Augustus chose negotiation over revenge. The return of the captured legionary standards in 20 BCE, stage-managed as a triumph, was in reality a diplomatic compromise with a power Rome had concluded it could not conquer. For three hundred years afterward, the Euphrates functioned as something like an accepted international border, with buffer kingdoms - Armenia above all - managed by both sides through a sophisticated apparatus of client kingship, royal marriages, and negotiated succession. This was a model Rome had never needed to develop in the west, where conquest sufficed. In the east, Parthia forced Rome to invent a more complex kind of statecraft.

Cultural and commercial absorption followed the armies and the envoys. Silk reached Rome through Parthian middlemen and drove the Roman elite to a spending spree so extravagant that Pliny the Elder complained it was bleeding the empire dry. Parthian fashion - trousers, long sleeves, high boots - migrated westward with the cavalry that wore it. By late antiquity, the Roman emperor himself was appearing in diadem and embroidered robes that would have been recognizable at the court of Ctesiphon.

Religion traveled the same routes. Mithraism, the mystery cult that spread through the Roman army in the second and third centuries CE and eventually maintained temples from Hadrian's Wall to the Syrian desert, drew on Iranian religious traditions that had matured in the Parthian world. The figure of Mithras, the bull-slaying saviour, wore Parthian dress: the trousers, the Phrygian cap, the flowing cloak. For two and a half centuries, Roman soldiers knelt in underground chapels before an image styled in the clothing of their ancestral enemies.

Rediscovering the Arsacids

For most of the last two thousand years, the Parthians were a rumor. They had no Herodotus, no Livy, no Sima Qian to tell their story from within. What survived came from their enemies - Roman historians writing of defeats and revenges, Armenian chroniclers recording the deeds of a junior branch, Chinese envoys describing a distant market, and above all the Sasanians, whose official contempt became the default verdict of the medieval Islamic historians who inherited the Iranian tradition.

Rediscovery began, as so many rediscoveries do, with coins. From the eighteenth century onward, European collectors and numismatists began to assemble cabinets of Arsacid silver tetradrachms and bronze drachms, and slowly to sort them into a dynasty. The names read off the Greek legends - Phraates, Orodes, Vologases - could then be matched with the fragmentary notices in Roman and Greek authors. By the end of the nineteenth century, something like a complete king list had emerged, albeit still full of gaps and question marks.

The twentieth century added dirt and stone. French and later Italian excavations at Susa uncovered Parthian administrative quarters. Russian and then Soviet archaeologists dug at Nisa in Turkmenistan, the dynastic heartland of the Arsacids, and brought up thousands of ostraca - potsherds with ink inscriptions - recording wine deliveries, estate accounts, and personal names in the Parthian language. These were not the grand chronicles the Sasanians had suppressed, but they were something perhaps more valuable: the everyday paperwork of an empire that had actually existed.

At Dura-Europos on the Euphrates, Yale-led excavations in the 1920s and 1930s uncovered a town that had passed from Parthian to Roman to Sasanian rule, its walls layered with frescoes, synagogues, churches, and mithraea. Hatra, in what is now northern Iraq, revealed a Parthian-era caravan city with temples and statues of its priest-kings wearing the full regalia of the Arsacid world. The great site of Ctesiphon itself, with the soaring brick arch of the Taq Kasra, had long stood visible on the Tigris; but it was only with systematic excavation that the scale of the Parthian and early Sasanian capital became clear.

Meanwhile, scholars trained in Iranian languages were reading Parthian inscriptions, Manichaean Parthian hymns, and the Parthian documents preserved in Central Asian Buddhist libraries. A literature that had supposedly never existed turned out to have survived, scattered and disguised, in the archives of other religions and other empires.

What has emerged from all this work, over the past century, is a dynasty that looks nothing like the Sasanian caricature. The Arsacids were not a provincial warlord family who stumbled into power. They built and held together, for nearly five centuries, the largest non-Chinese state in Eurasia. They made the Silk Road work. They shaped the military cultures of Rome and Iran alike. They gave Armenia its royal house and its entry into Christianity. They governed a religiously plural, linguistically diverse, politically decentralized empire with a light enough touch to endure longer than the Roman principate or the Han dynasty.

Key Figures & Events

Ardashir I, the Sasanian founder who defeated Artabanus IV in 224 CE, stands at the center of the Parthian afterlife - not because he destroyed the empire, but because he authored the version of its history that almost everyone else believed. His rock reliefs at Naqsh-e Rustam set the template. The great noble houses - Suren, Karen, Mihran, Ispahbudhan - embody the other half of the story: an aristocracy that survived its own dynasty and carried Parthian institutions forward under new kings. Tiridates III of Armenia, an Arsacid ruling after the Arsacids had fallen in Iran, turned a Parthian throne into the first Christian state. And the modern archaeologists at Nisa, Dura-Europos, and Hatra - though they will never have a rock relief of their own - are the ones who finally gave the Parthians back their voice.

Analysis

History does not always reward the empires that deserve remembering. The Parthians governed longer than Rome's western empire, influenced a wider swath of Eurasia than most of their contemporaries, and held their own against every power that came at them from east or west. Yet, because they lost the final war and because their successors had a story to tell, they became the forgotten middle chapter of Iranian history. Their afterlife is a lesson in the politics of memory: that who writes the chronicle matters as much as who wins the battle, and that silence can be engineered. The Parthians' rediscovery in our own time is also a reminder that silence can be undone - that coins in a drawer, potsherds in a trench, and frescoes in a desert town can, given enough patience, outvote the propaganda of kings.

Quick Summary

- The Sasanians systematically downplayed Parthian achievements, portraying the Arsacid centuries as a period of fragmentation and weakness.
- The great Parthian noble houses - Suren, Karen, Mihran - survived the dynastic change and continued to dominate Iranian military and political life under the Sasanians.
- The Armenian branch of the Arsacid dynasty ruled until 428 CE and presided over Armenia's conversion to Christianity around 301 CE.
- Parthian influence persisted in Georgia, the Kushan realm, Indo-Parthian kingdoms, and along the Silk Road long after 224 CE.
- Rome absorbed Parthian cavalry tactics, diplomatic practices, luxury trade, fashion, and religious currents, most notably Mithraism.
- Modern recovery of the Parthians began with numismatics and accelerated with twentieth-century excavations at Nisa, Dura-Europos, Hatra, and Ctesiphon.
- The Parthians held together the largest non-Chinese state in Eurasia for nearly five centuries and made the Silk Road a functioning system.

The Parthian afterlife is still being written. Every season, an excavation in Iran, Iraq, or Central Asia produces another seal, another ostracon, another inscription that fills in a blank the Sasanians worked hard to create. The empire that rode between Rome and China, that shaped the medieval world without ever being credited for it, is slowly being returned to the place it occupied in its own time: not a gap between greater civilizations, but one of the great civilizations itself. It took almost two thousand years. The riders of the forgotten empire are finally being remembered.

A Note on Sources

The Parthian Empire presents the historian with a paradox that is almost perverse in its irony: one of the ancient world's most powerful and enduring states left almost nothing of its own written record. The Arsacids ruled for nearly five centuries, yet no Parthian court chronicle, royal annals, or official history has survived - and in all likelihood, none was ever composed in a form recognizable to us. We are left to reconstruct an empire largely through the eyes of its enemies, its neighbors, and the occasional sympathetic outsider.

The bulk of our literary evidence comes from Greek and Roman sources. Strabo, Pliny the Elder, Plutarch, Cassius Dio, and Justin (in his epitome of Pompeius Trogus) provide the skeletal framework for Parthian political and military history, though each writes with his own biases, gaps, and agendas. Plutarch's account of Carrhae is vivid and indispensable, but it is Caesar's Rome that occupies the center of his moral universe. Cassius Dio is invaluable for the later Roman-Parthian wars but writes at a considerable remove from events. Justin's epitome of Trogus preserves much that would otherwise be lost, yet it is frustratingly compressed precisely at the moments we most want detail. These sources must be read critically, with constant awareness that for Roman authors, Parthia is above all a foil - a measure of Roman virtue, failure, or ambition.

The Parthian royal inscriptions that do survive are sparse and formulaic. The Arsacid coinage tradition, however, is an exception of real importance: the long numismatic sequence of Parthian coins, studied by scholars such as David Sellwood and more recently by Vesta Sarkhosh Curtis and Michael Alram, offers a largely independent line of evidence for dynastic chronology, royal titulature, and even shifts in royal ideology. Coins are often the only source from which we can establish the sequence of rulers in contested periods.

Archaeological evidence has grown considerably in recent decades, though the picture remains uneven. Excavations at Nisa, the early Arsacid heartland in modern Turkmenistan, produced the remarkable Nisa rhyta and a archive of Parthian-language ostraca - administrative documents of enormous value. Work at Dura-Europos on the middle Euphrates, conducted primarily by Yale University and the French Academy in the early twentieth century, illuminated life in a provincial Parthian garrison city with extraordinary detail. Seleucia-on-the-Tigris and Ctesiphon remain comparatively understudied relative to their historical importance, a gap that reflects the complex political circumstances surrounding fieldwork in modern Iraq and Iran.

The Parthian ostraca from Nisa, published and analyzed by Igor Diakonoff, Vladimir Livshits, and their successors, represent our most substantial body of Parthian-language documentary evidence. The Aramaic parchments from Avroman, the Parthian documents from Dura, and inscriptions in Middle Iranian languages from across the empire supplement these, though the total corpus remains slender. For Mesopotamian evidence, the cuneiform astronomical diaries from Babylon - not primarily historical documents but scientific records - preserve incidental notices of political events of remarkable precision, and have been mined carefully by scholars including R. J. van der Spek.

Chinese sources deserve particular mention. The *Shiji* of Sima Qian and the *Hanshu* offer accounts of early diplomatic and commercial contact with Anxi - the Chinese rendering of Arsacid - that are independent of the Greco-Roman tradition entirely. These passages, brief as they are, are essential for situating the Parthian empire within its full Eurasian context and for understanding the dynamics of the Silk Road trade.

For modern scholarship, the field has been transformed over the past half century. Nikolaus Debevoise's *A Political History of Parthia* (1938) long served as the standard reference and remains useful, though much has been revised since. Józef Wolski devoted a career to Parthian political history. Malcolm Colledge's work on Parthian art opened systematic study of the empire's visual culture. More recently, the volume *Parthia and Rome* edited by Monika Schuol, Udo Hartmann, and Andreas Luther, the contributions of Edward Dąbrowa, and the comprehensive survey by Vesta Sarkhosh Curtis and Sarah Stewart have collectively reshaped the field. Jason Olson, Bruno Jacobs, and Gunnar Dumke have advanced our understanding of Parthian administration and court culture. The Cambridge History of Iran remains an essential reference.

Where sources conflict - as they frequently do on questions of dynastic chronology, the outcome of particular campaigns, or the internal politics of the Arsacid court - I have tried to signal the uncertainty rather than paper over it with false confidence. The Parthian Empire deserves to be understood on its own terms, not simply as a backdrop to Roman ambition. That we must pursue that understanding through such imperfect and partial evidence is not a reason for despair, but for a kind of scholarly humility that the Arsacids, lords of an empire that outlasted most, might have appreciated.

Chronology

c. 247 BCE
Arsaces I leads the Parni into the Seleucid satrapy of Parthia, founding the Arsacid dynasty.
c. 238 BCE

Arsaces defeats the Seleucid satrap Andragoras and consolidates control of Parthia proper.
171-132 BCE
Reign of Mithridates I, who transforms the Parthian kingdom into an empire stretching from the Euphrates to Bactria.
141 BCE
Mithridates I enters Seleucia-on-the-Tigris and is crowned King of Kings.
123-88 BCE
Reign of Mithridates II the Great, who stabilizes the empire and receives the first Chinese embassy under Han Wudi.
53 BCE
The Parthian general Surena annihilates Crassus's Roman army at the Battle of Carrhae.
40-38 BCE
Parthian forces under Pacorus briefly overrun Roman Syria before being defeated by Ventidius.
36 BCE
Mark Antony's invasion of Media Atropatene ends in disaster and heavy Roman losses.
20 BCE
Phraates IV returns the captured Roman standards to Augustus, a diplomatic triumph commemorated across Rome.
63 CE
The Treaty of Rhandeia establishes an Arsacid branch on the Armenian throne under Roman acknowledgment.
c. 1st century CE
The Indo-Parthian king Gondophares rules a kingdom spanning parts of eastern Iran, Afghanistan, and northwest India.
114-117 CE
Emperor Trajan invades Mesopotamia, briefly creating Roman provinces of Armenia and Mesopotamia.

117 CE
Hadrian abandons Trajan's eastern conquests, restoring the Euphrates frontier.
161-166 CE
War with Rome under Vologases IV; Lucius Verus's forces sack Seleucia and Ctesiphon, returning with the Antonine Plague.
197-198 CE
Septimius Severus invades Parthia and sacks Ctesiphon, annexing northern Mesopotamia to Rome.
216-217 CE
Caracalla attacks Parthia under diplomatic pretense; Artabanus IV defeats Macrinus at the Battle of Nisibis.
c. 208-224 CE
Civil war between Vologases VI and Artabanus IV weakens the Arsacid state.
224 CE
Ardashir I of the House of Sasan defeats and kills Artabanus IV at the Battle of Hormozdgan, ending the Arsacid Empire.
226 CE
Ardashir crowned King of Kings at Ctesiphon, founding the Sasanian Empire.
c. 428 CE
The Arsacid line of Armenian kings, last heirs of the Parthian royal tradition, is extinguished.

Further Reading

The literature on the Parthian Empire is more substantial than its relative obscurity in popular history might suggest, though it remains skewed toward specialist journals and edited volumes rather than accessible single-author narratives. What follows is a selective guide for readers wishing to go deeper, organized by theme.

General Histories and Overviews

The most comprehensive modern survey in English is The Parthian Empire and Its Religions and related volumes in the series edited by Vesta Sarkhosh Curtis and Sarah Stewart (The Age of the Parthians, I.B. Tauris, 2007), which brings together leading specialists on art, religion, numismatics, and history. Nikolaus Debevoise's A Political History of Parthia (University of Chicago Press, 1938) remains a useful reference despite its age. For a concise and reliable overview, Geo Widengren's chapter in the Cambridge History of Iran, vol. 3 (1983) is still worth consulting. Josef Wiesehöfer's Ancient Persia (I.B. Tauris, 1996) situates the Arsacids within the longer sweep of Iranian history accessibly and intelligently.

Primary Sources in Translation

Plutarch's Life of Crassus - available in numerous editions, including the Penguin Fall of the Roman Republic - remains the essential account of Carrhae and Parthian military methods. Justin's Epitome of the Philippic History of Pompeius Trogus, translated by J. C. Yardley (Scholars Press, 1994), preserves the most sustained ancient narrative of Arsacid dynastic history. For Chinese perspectives, the relevant passages from the Shiji and Hanshu are collected and translated in Xinru Liu's The Silk Road in World History (Oxford University Press, 2010).

Military History

For the Parthian way of war and its impact on Rome, N. C. Debevoise's work remains foundational, but it should be supplemented with Philip Rance's articles on cavalry and the articles collected in New Perspectives on the Later Roman Empire (various). Rose Mary Sheldon's Rome's Wars in Parthia (Vallentine Mitchell, 2010) offers a sustained military-historical treatment.

For Carrhae specifically, the literature is extensive; Gareth Sampson's The Defeat of Rome (Pen & Sword, 2008) provides a readable reconstruction.

Numismatics

David Sellwood's An Introduction to the Coinage of Parthia (2nd ed., Spink, 1980) is the standard typological reference. Michael Alram's work, including contributions to the Sylloge Nummorum Graecorum series, advances the field considerably. The catalogue Faces of the Parthian World (British Museum, 2010), edited by Vesta Sarkhosh Curtis and Michael Alram, is both scholarly and visually illuminating.

Archaeology and Material Culture

Malcolm Colledge's Parthian Art (Thames & Hudson, 1977) opened systematic study of Arsacid visual culture and remains a foundational text. For Nisa, the site reports by the Italian-Turkmen Archaeological Mission (MAIKI) are the essential reference; accessible summaries appear in several of the Curtis and Stewart volumes. For Dura-Europos, the original Yale excavation reports are supplemented by Ted Kaizer's edited volume The Variety of Local Religious Life in the Near East (Brill, 2008) and Simon James's The Roman Military Base at Dura-Europos (Oxford University Press, 2019).

Trade and the Silk Road

Xinru Liu's The Silk Road in World History (Oxford University Press, 2010) is the best single-volume introduction. Valerie Hansen's The Silk Road: A New History (Oxford University Press, 2012) is excellent on the archaeological evidence. For the Parthian role specifically, see the relevant chapters in Trade, Commerce, and the State in the Roman World, edited by Andrew Wilson and Alan Bowman (Oxford University Press, 2018).

Religion and Culture

Frantz Grenet's work on Zoroastrianism and the Iranian religious world is indispensable; his articles are scattered across specialist journals but consistently illuminating. For the Hellenistic-Iranian cultural synthesis, Susan Sherwin-White and Amélie Kuhrt's From Samarkhand to Sardis (Duckworth, 1993) remains essential reading, though its primary focus is the Seleucid period. Philippe Gignoux's work on Mazdaism in the Parthian period is available in French and in English translation in collected volumes.

The Roman-Parthian Frontier

Susan P. Mattern's Rome and the Enemy (University of California Press, 1999) is superb on Roman strategic thinking about Parthia. Everett Wheeler's articles on Roman frontier strategy in the east are important for specialists. For the Armenian dimension, see Mack Chahin's The Kingdom of Armenia (Curzon, 2001) and the relevant chapters in the Cambridge Ancient History, vol. 10 and 11.

The End of the Arsacids and the Sasanian Transition

Touraj Daryaee's Sasanian Persia: The Rise and Fall of an Empire (I.B. Tauris, 2009) is the best starting point for understanding what came after - and what the Sasanians inherited and transformed. Matthew Canepa's The Two Eyes of the Earth (University of California Press, 2009) examines the long competition between Iranian and Roman imperial ideologies in ways that illuminate the Arsacid legacy.